MY FIRST STEPS
IN ISLAM

Abd Ar-Rahman bin
Abd Al-Kareem Ash-Sheha

© **Islamic Guidance Community Awareness Association in Rabwah, 2021**
King Fahd National Library Cataloging-in-Publication Data

Al-Sheha, Abdul Rahman Bin Abdulkareen

My First Steps In Islam. / Al-Sheha, Abdul Rahman Bin Abdulkareen - 2..-
Riyadh, 2021

92 p; 15.3 x 19.6 cm

ISBN: 978-603-8352-47-2

1- Al-Islam   I-Title
210 dc   1443/5051

L.D. no. 1443/5051
ISBN: 978-603-8352-47-2

In the name of Allah,
the Beneficent, the Merciful

Dear Reader,

Islam is a complete and integral Divine religion and way of life. It has a complete code of ethics for a happy life, as well as a peaceful and tranquil life after death.
Islam is free from all imperfections and defects.
Any deviant or abnormal behavior observed in a Muslim should have no bearing on Islam, none whatsoever.
The reason for such deviant behavior is generally a poor understanding of the faith, and in other cases, weak faith that leads to the person going astray from what is proper and noble.
It is unjust and unreasonable for Islam to be assessed or evaluated based on any individuals' behavior or attitudes, with the exception of the Prophet Muhammad, who is the best example and role model for all humans.

TABLE OF CONTENTS

INTRODUCTION	08
THE SHAHAADATAYN	12
BELIEF IN THE ANGELS	18
BELIEF IN THE BOOKS OF ALLAH	22
BELIEF IN ALLAH'S MESSENGERS	26
BELIEF IN THE LAST DAY	28
BELIEF IN QADAA´ AND QADAR	32
WHAT ONE SHOULD DO AFTER PRONOUNCING THE SHAHAADATAYN	36
ZAKAH	50
THE FAST (SIYAAM) OF RAMADAN	52
HAJJ	54
THE WORSHIP OF ALLAH	58
THE COMMANDMENTS OF ISLAM	60
SOME PROHIBITIONS CONCERNING FOOD, DRINK AND CLOTHING	70
VARIOUS SUPPLICATIONS, WORDS OF REMEMBRANCE, AND ISLAMIC ETIQUETTES	72
BROTHERLY ADVICE	76

FOREWORD

This book has been conceived, prepared and designed by the Osoul Centre. All photos used in the book belong to the Osoul Centre. The Centre hereby permits all Sunni Muslims to reprint and publish the book in any method and format on condition that 1) acknowledgement of the Osoul Centre is clearly stated on all editions; and 2) no alteration or amendment of the text is introduced without reference to the Osoul Centre. In the case of reprinting this book, the Centre strongly recommends maintaining high quality.

☎ +966 11 445 4900

📠 +966 11 497 0126

✉ P.O.Box 29465, Riyadh 11457

@ osoul@rabwah.sa

🌐 www.osoulcenter.com

All praise be to God, the Lord of all the worlds, the Creator of the heavens and earth and all creatures living in them. May God grant peace and blessings to Prophet Muhammad, God's final Messenger, whose message brought mercy to all mankind. May He also give His blessings to all the prophets and messengers whom He sent to guide mankind out of darkness and into light.

At the Osoul Centre for Islamic Advocacy, every new release that we produce gives us a great opportunity to interact with our readers. All our releases have the same overall objective; to present Islam to mankind, as it truly is. We aim to make people aware of Islam's fine aspects and profound teachings and to show clearly that it is the only faith that provides practical and effective solutions to all the problems faced by humanity. Islam gives clear and solid answers to all of the questions that have troubled people over many generations, such as: How did we come into existence and why do we exist? Where do we go from here? Furthermore, Islam is the only religion that requires its followers to love and respect all the prophets God sent, particularly Moses and Jesus (peace be upon them both).

We take great care to provide solid and rational proofs for our arguments, so as to give our readers the reassurance they need, and our releases also refute the accusations levelled against Islam and provide clarification to people's misunderstandings of Islamic teachings.

By God's grace, Islam is the fastest growing religion in our time, as confirmed by a study undertaken by the Pew Research Center[1], and our motive is to make this great divine faith known to all people.

This book, **My First Steps in Islam**, explains the basic tenets of the religion that every new convert, or more properly stated, revert, should be familiar with to best progress in their relationship with God. It covers a great many essential points in both matters of belief, as well as acts of worship, in a concise and easy to understand manner.

We hope that this book will be of benefit to Muslim readers, giving them clear knowledge of the rules of their religion in this area. We also hope that non-Muslim readers will gain an insight into the most essential aspects of the religion of Islam and will find this book interesting.

Executive Director

---

(1) "The Future of the Global Muslim Population", Pew Research Center, 27 January 2011, Available at http://goo.gl/k0FJ8Y

MY FIRST STEPS IN ISLAM

INTRODUCTION

All praise is due to Allah, the Lord of the worlds, and may Allah exalt the mention of His Prophet, and render him and his household safe and secure from all derogatory things.

I sincerely congratulate you for the guidance Allah has granted and favored you with. I ask Allah that He keeps us and all Muslims firm upon this great religion until we meet Him, without changing anything from it and not being put through trials.

Indeed a true Muslim feels great joy when someone accepts Islam, for he wishes well for others and wants them to live as he does himself: a life of comfort and delight with spiritual joy and mental stability. This can only result from implementing the teachings of Islam. Allah says:
"Whoever does good whether male or female and he is a believer, We will most certainly make him live a happy life, and We will most certainly give them their reward for the best of what they did." [16:97]

This is because Allah clarified the condition of those who do not believe in Allah and what He revealed. Allah says:
"And whoever turns away from My Reminder, verily, for him is a life of hardship, and We shall raise him up blind on the Day of Resurrection. He will say, 'O my Lord! Why have you raised me up blind, while [before] I had sight.' He [Allah] will say, 'Like this Our signs came to you, but you disregarded them, and so this Day, you will be neglected." [20:124-126]

A true Muslim wishes that they live happily forever in the Hereafter, whose delights are never-ending. Allah says:

"Verily those who believe and do righteous deeds shall have the Gardens of Firdaws for their entertainment. Therein they shall dwell [forever]. No desire will they have for removal there from." [18:107-108]

The end is inevitable: either eternal happiness or eternal remorse. Whoever dies upon disbelief - and refuge is sought in Allah - he will enter Hellfire for eternity. Allah says:
"Verily those who disbelieve from the people of the Book and the polytheists will abide in the Fire of Hell. They are the worst of creatures." [98:6]

Dear brother/sister, indeed it is a great blessing and favor of Allah that He has guided you to Islam and has saved you from disbelief, for there are many who have not been granted the guidance to realize the correct religion, as there are many who have realized that Islam is the true Religion but have not been granted the guidance to follow it. So you should thank Allah, my brother/sister, for this favor from Allah and this gift which He has given you. Ask Allah that He keeps you firm upon this religion until you meet Him. Allah says:
"They consider it a favor to you that they have accepted Islam. Say, 'Do not consider your Islam a favor to me. Rather, Allah has conferred favor upon you that He has guided you to the faith, if you should be truthful.'" [49:17]

We are all in need of Allah. Allah says:
"O Mankind! It is you who stand in need of Allah. you are those in need of Allah, while Allah is the Free of need, the Praiseworthy." [35:15]

Allah does not need us: He neither benefits from our obedience and worship, nor is He harmed by our disbelief and disobedience. Allah says:
"If you disbelieve, then verily Allah is not in need of you. He likes not disbelief for His slaves. And if you are grateful, He approves it for you; and no bearer of burdens will bear the burden of another. Then to your Lord is your return, and He will inform you about what you used to do." [39:7]

The Messenger of Allah ﷺ said in a Hadeeth Qudsi[1]:
"Allah said: 'O My slaves! I have forbidden dhulm (oppression) for Myself, and I have made it forbidden amongst you, so do not oppress one another. O My

---

(1) Hadeeth Qudsi: Hadeeth is a narration of the speech, actions, tacit approvals, and characteristics of the Prophet ﷺ. Hadeeth Qudsi is a Hadeeth in which the Prophet ﷺ narrates from Allah in the first person (I).

slaves, all of you are astray except those whom I have guided, so seek guidance from Me and I shall guide you. O My slaves, all of you are hungry except those whom I have fed, so seek food from Me and I shall feed you. O My slaves, all of you are naked except those whom I have clothed, so seek clothing from Me and I shall clothe you. O My slaves, you commit sins by day and by night, and I forgive all sins, so seek forgiveness from Me and I shall forgive you. O My slaves, you will not attain harming Me so as to harm me, and you will not attain benefiting Me so as to benefit Me. O My slaves, if the first of you and the last of you, and the humans of you and the Jinn[2] of you, were all as pious as the most pious heart of any individual amongst you, then this would not increase My Kingdom an iota. O My slaves, if the first of you and the last of you, and the humans of you and the Jinn of you, were all as wicked as the most wicked heart of any individual amongst you, then this would not decrease My Kingdom an iota. O My slaves, if the first of you and the last of you, and the humans of you and the Jinn of you, were all to stand together in one place and ask of Me, and I were to give everyone what he requested, then that would not decrease what I possess, except what is decreased of the Ocean when a needle is dipped into it. O My slaves, it is but your deeds that I account for you and then recompense you for. So he who finds good, let him praise Allah, and he who finds other than that, let him blame no one but himself.'" (Muslim #2577)

In order to become a Muslim, there are no specific religious rituals or customs that you need to perform, neither in specific areas, nor in front of people. This is due to the fact that in Islam man has direct relationship with his Lord without any intermediaries.

---

(2) Jinn: A creation from the unseen having free will like the humans, created from a smokeless flame of fire.

Also, you don't need to exert great efforts [to enter its folds]. You merely need to utter a few words, which are easy on the tongue, while understanding their great meanings.

One who has decided to become Muslim should utter Shahaadatayn'[3] in order to enter the fold of Islam, which is:
"Ash-hadu an laa ilaaha ill-Allah, wa ashhadu anna Muhammadan 'abd-ullahi wa rasooluh".

Meaning: I testify that there is no true god except Allah, and I testify that Muhammad is His slave and Messenger.

This statement is the key to enter Islam. Whoever utters it shuns all other religions besides Islam and all beliefs which differ with it. Through this statement, he receives the rights which all Muslims receive, and he must fulfill the rights which all Muslims fulfill. His wealth, honor and life become sacred, except for that which is prescribed by Islam.

It is true that one is considered a Muslim by his apparent actions, but only Allah knows what is truly in the hearts, so what are the meanings of the Shahaadatayn?

---
(3) Shahaadatayn: Literally, the Two Testimonies of Faith.

MY FIRST STEPS IN ISLAM

01 THE SHAHAADATAYN

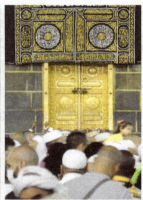

The name, "Allah", written in block calligraphy

THE TWO TESTIMONIES OF FAITH

These are the testimonies that no one has the right to be worshipped but Allah, and that Muhammad is His slave and messenger. This is a verbal pillar of Islam, but one must also follow it with belief and action. This is the key to enter Islam.

THE MEANING OF THE FIRST TESTIMONY:

This is the phrase of Tawheed[1]. For this concept, Allah brought the creation into being, and for this concept He created Paradise and Hellfire. Allah says:

"And I have created neither the Jinn nor mankind except to worship Me." [51:56]

This is the belief to which all Prophets and Messengers called their peoples, may Allah praise them and keep them safe from all evil. Allah says:

"And we have not sent before you any messenger except that We have revealed to him that there is no god that is worshipped in truth except Me, so worship and obey Me." [21:25]

The first testimony, that none has the right to be worshipped but Allah, includes the following meanings:

- Allah is the Creator of all that exists. Allah says:
  "Such is Allah, your Lord! None has the right to be worshipped but Him, the Creator of all things. So worship and obey Him Alone, and He is the Guardian over all things." [6:102]

---

(1) Tawheed: The concept of the Oneness of Allah.

- Allah is the Proprietor of all that exists, and the Disposer of all affairs[2]. Allah says:

  "Surely, His is the Creation and Commandment. Blessed be Allah, the Lord of all that exists!" [7:54]

- Allah is the One who deserves to be worshipped.[3] Allah says:

  "Unquestionably, to Allah belongs whoever is in the heavens and whoever is on the earth. And those who invoke other than Allah do not actually follow His alleged partners. They follow not except assumption, and they only invent lies." [10:66]

- To Him belong the beautiful names and perfect attributes. Far removed is He from every imperfection.[4]

  Allah says:

  "And all the Most Beautiful Names belong to Allah, so call on Him by them, and leave the company of those who belie or deny His Names. They will be requited for what they used to do." [7:180]

THE CONDITIONS OF THE TESTIMONY:

It is not enough to merely say this testimony for it to be accepted by Allah. It is a key to the gates of Paradise, but in order for the key to work, it needs to have the right ridges. This Testimony must meet the following conditions for it to be accepted by Allah:

1. **KNOWLEDGE:** This comprises knowing that all things worshipped besides Allah are false. There is no god worshipped in truth except Allah, even if it be a prophet, a messenger or an angel. Allah is the only One Who deserves all types of worship, such as prayer, supplication, hope, sacrifice, fasting, etc.

   Whoever assigns any act of worship to other than Allah while that person intends to worship or aggrandize the one who he assigned it to, has committed an act of disbelief, even if he uttered the two testimonies.

---

(2) Points one and two are known as Tawheed ar-Ruboobiyyah, or the Oneness of Allah's Lordship. This is the belief that there is no Creator, Provider, Sustainer, and Owner except for Allah.

(3) This is the concept known as Tawheed al-Uloohiyyah, or the Oneness of Allah in His worship.

(4) This concept is known as Tawheed al-Asmaa´ was-Sifaat, that Allah has the Best Names and Attributes, and that there are none equal or comparable to them.

MY FIRST STEPS IN ISLAM

Allah is the only One Who has the right to legislate, whether it be in matters concerning worship or those concerning human relations; in both individual and public matters.

Muhammad ﷺ

2. CERTAINTY: The heart must be firmly certain of the meaning of the two testimonies. Certainty is the opposite of doubt, so there is no room for a person to doubt or hesitate in his belief. Allah says:

"The believers are only those who have believed in Allah and His Messenger, and afterward doubt not, and strive with their wealth and their lives for the Cause of Allah. Those are the truthful." [49:15]

3. ACCEPTANCE: One should accept the testimony fully, and not reject it.[5] Allah says:

"Truly, when it was said to them, 'There is no true deity worshipped except Allah,' they puff themselves up with pride in denial." [37:35]

4. SUBMISSION, obedience and acting upon all what the testimonies necessitate.[6] A person must do what Allah ordered and abstain from what He prohibited. Allah says:

"And whosoever submits his face to Allah, while he is a Muhsin[7] then he has grasped the most trustworthy handhold. And to Allah return all matters for decision." [31:22]

5. TRUTHFULNESS: One must be truthful in professing the testimonies.[8] Allah says:

"They say with their tongues what is not within their hearts." [48:11]

---

(5) It is not sufficient that a person knows what the Shahaadah means and believes it with certainty. Rather he must accept it by pronouncing it, and accepts to become a Muslim.
(6) It is not sufficient that a person knows what the Shahaadah means and believes it with certainty, accepts it by pronouncing it and accepts to become a Muslim. Rather, he must also act according to it.
(7) Muhsin: Literally, a person who does something well. Here it means one who does righteous deeds sincerely for Allah, according to the method the Prophet of Allah mentions both submission to Allah along with doing righteous deeds, and if a person does these, he has grasped the Shahaadah.
(8) Even though a person may be doing all these things on the outside, he might be hiding disbelief in his heart, like the Hypocrites.

6. **SINCERITY OF WORSHIP:** One must sincerely dedicate all acts of worship to Allah alone.[9] Allah says:

"And they were not commanded except to worship Allah, following the religion purely and sincerely for Him, turning away from other religions." [98:5]

7. **LOVE:** One must love the testimonies and all that they necessitate. He must love Allah, His Messenger, and His righteous servants. He must show enmity towards all who show enmity to Allah and His Messenger. He must prefer what Allah and His Messenger love, even if it differs from his desires. Allah says:

"Say: If your fathers, your sons, your brothers, your wives, your kindred, the wealth that you have gained, the commerce in which you fear a decline, and the dwellings in which you delight are dearer to you than Allah and His Messenger, and fighting in His Cause, then wait until Allah brings about His Decision. And Allah does not guide the defiantly disobedient people." [9:24]

These testimonies also necessitate that Allah is the only One Who has the right to legislate, whether it be in matters concerning worship or those concerning human relations, in both individual and public matters.

The act of making something prohibited or lawful is for Allah alone. His Messenger merely explained and clarified Allah's commandments. Allah says:

"And whatsoever the Messenger gives you, take it, and whatsoever he forbids you, refrain from it." [59:7]

THE MEANING OF THE SECOND TESTIMONY, THAT 'MUHAMMAD IS HIS MESSENGER'

To bear witness that Muhammad the Messenger of Allah necessitates the following:

1. To believe that he is a Messenger, and that he is last of the Messengers; no Messenger will come after him. Allah says:

"Muhammad is not the father of any man among you, but he is the Messenger of Allah and the last of the Prophets." [33:40]

2. To believe that he is infallible in the teachings he conveyed from Allah. Allah, the Exalted, says:

---

(9) It may be that one fulfills all the previous conditions, but he directs worship to other than Allah at times, like supplicating to the dead, etc. Such a person has not made his worship purely for Allah.

MY FIRST STEPS IN ISLAM

"Nor does he speak of his own inclination. It is only an Revelation that is revealed to him." [53:3-4]

As for the affairs of this world, he was a human, and he had his own opinions. The Prophet ﷺ said:

"Indeed I am only a human. It may be that a claimant comes to me with a dispute, and due to one of them being more convincing in speech than the other, I may rule in his favor. Whoever was ruled in his favor while he is wrong, what he is receiving without right is only a portion of the Hellfire, so let him take it or leave it." [Muslim]

3. To believe that he is a Messenger to all creation; to Jinn and to humans until the Final Hour. Allah says:

"And We have not sent you [O Muhammad ﷺ] except to all of mankind, as a giver of glad tidings and a warner, but most people know not." [34:28]

4. To obey the Prophet ﷺ in what he ordered, to believe in everything he said, and to refrain from what he forbade and warned against. Allah says:

"And whatsoever the Messenger gives you, take it, and whatsoever he forbids you, refrain from it." [59:7]

5. To follow and adhere to the Prophet's ﷺ Sunnah, without innovating matters in it. Allah, the Exalted, says:

"Say [O Muhammad ﷺ]: If you truly love Allah then follow my example, Allah will love you and forgive you your sins. And Allah is Oft-Forgiving, Most Merciful." [3:31]

When one fulfills the conditions of the Shahadah, he would free himself from worshipping man and devote all acts of worship to the Creator of man. This would lead one to being independent.

The Merits Of Iman: A sense of security through the knowledge that there is someone to turn to in times of hardships.

Ther is no other God of worship except Allah, and Muhammad is His Messenger

THE MERITS OF IMAN (BELIEF) IN Allah

1. When one fulfills the conditions of the Shahadah, he would free himself from worshipping man and devote all acts of worship to the Creator of man. This would lead one to being independent. Allah says:

"Say: 'Then have you considered what you invoke besides Allah? If Allah intended me harm, are they removers of His harm; or if He intended me mercy, are they withholders of His mercy?' Say, 'Sufficient for me is Allah; upon Him [alone] rely the [wise] reliers.'" [39:38]

2. Peace of heart, mind and soul. Allah says:

"Those who believe and whose hearts find rest in the remembrance of Allah, Verily, in the remembrance of Allah do hearts find rest." [13:28]

3. Sense of security through the knowledge that there is someone to turn to in times of hardships. Allah says:

"And when harm touches you upon the sea, those that you call upon besides Him vanish from you except Him. But when He brings you safely to land, you turn away [from Him]. And man is ever ungrateful." [17:67]

4. The feeling of spiritual joy in worshipping Allah. This is due to the fact that the goal which he is trying to achieve (Jannah) cannot be reached except after death. So you see him persistently striving to achieve this goal by doing righteous deeds, rendering all acts of worship sincerely and purely to Allah alone. Allah says:

"Say: 'Verily, my prayer, my sacrifice, my living and my dying are for Allah, the Lord of the worlds. He has no partner. And of this I have been commanded, and I am the first of the Muslims.'" [6:162-163]

5. The guidance and success which is granted by Allah to those that believe in Him. Allah says:

"…and whosoever has faith in Allah, He guides his heart." [64:11]

6. The love of doing righteous deeds and its propagation amongst the masses. Allah says:

"So whosoever does good equal to the weight of an atom shall see it." [99:7]

The Prophet ﷺ said:

"Indeed the one who leads another to do a righteous deed is like the one who actually does it[10]." (Tirmidhi #2670)

---

(10) He will receive the same reward.

02 BELIEF IN THE ANGELS

It is to believe that the Angels are from the creation of Allah; no-one knows their exact number except Him. They are from the unseen world. Allah created them to worship and obey Him. Allah says:

"Never would the Messiah disdain to be a servant of Allah, nor would the angels near [to Him]. And whoever disdains His worship and is arrogant - He will gather them to Himself all together." [4:172]

The Angels are a creation of Allah which He created from light. The Messenger of Allah ﷺ said:

"The angels were created from light, the Jinn were created from a smokeless flame of fire, and Adam was created from what was described to you (in the Qur`an: black dry clay)." [Muslim]

Belief in the Angels it is to believe that the angels are from the creation of Allah; no-one knows their exact number except Him. They are from the unseen world. Allah created them to worship and obey Him.

Allah created them to do certain tasks; which they execute. Allah says:

"[The angels say], 'There is not among us any except that he has a known position. And indeed, we are those who line up [for prayer]. And indeed, we are those who exalt Allah.'" [37:164-166]

Allah has informed us of some of their names, such as Jibreel (Gabriel), Mikaa`eel (Michael), and Israafeel (Rafael). Allah says: "Whoever is an enemy to Allah and His Angels and His Messengers and Gabriel and Michael - then indeed, Allah is an enemy to the disbelievers." [2:98]

Jibreel is the angel who descends with the revelation upon the messengers, who convey it to their nations. Allah says:

"The Trustworthy Spirit has brought it down. Upon your heart, (O Muhammad ﷺ), that you may be of the warners." [26:193-194]

Meekaa`eel is assigned with the task of distributing rain and vegetation, while Israafeel has been assigned the task of blowing the horn that signals the events of the Last Day. He will blow it for the first time, and all would be struck with terror. Allah says:

"And [mention] the Day the Horn will be blown, and whoever is in the heavens and whoever is on the earth will be terrified except whom Allah wills." [27:87]

Thereafter, he would blow the trumpet two more times on the Day of Judgment; the second with which all would die, and the third with which all would be resurrected and brought back to life. Allah says:

"And the Horn will be blown, and whoever is in the heavens and whoever is on the earth will fall dead except whom Allah wills. Then it will be blown again, and at once they will be standing, looking on." [39:68]

Among the angels is also the Angel of Death and his helpers. Allah says:

"And He is the subjugator over His slaves, and He sends over you guardian-angels until, when death comes to one of you, Our messengers take him, and they do not fail [in their duties]. Then they are returned to Allah, their true Lord. Unquestionably, His is the judgment, and He is the swiftest of accountants." [6:61-62]

Among them are also those who bear the Throne of Allah, and those who are also close to Him. Allah says:

"And the angels are at its edges. And there will bear the Throne of your Lord above them, that Day, eight [of them]." [69:17]

Some have been assigned tasks in Jannah, while others have been assigned tasks in Hellfire. Allah says:

"O you who have believed, protect yourselves and your families from a Fire, whose fuel is people and stones, over which are angels, harsh and severe; they do not disobey Allah in what He commands them but do what they are commanded." [66:6]

Among them are those who have been assigned the task to protect humans. Allah says:

"For each [person] there are angels in succession, before and behind him. They guard him by the Command of Allah." [13:11]

Some of them record man's deeds. Allah says:

"And indeed, (appointed) over you are keepers[1], noble and recording; They know whatever you do." [82:10-12]

- Allah created Angels to worship Him. He says:
"To Him belongs whoever is in the heavens and the earth. And those near Him are not prevented by arrogance from His worship, nor do they tire. They exalt [Him] night and day and do not slacken." [21:19-20]

No one knows their exact number except Allah. Allah says: "And We have not made the keepers of the Fire except angels. And We have not made their number except as a trial for those who disbelieve." [74:31]

Whoever desires to learn more on this subject may read books (which are based on the Qur'an and authentic Sunnah) which talk about the angels and their duties.

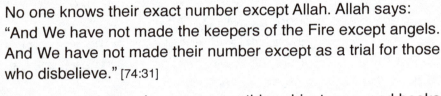

Merits of belief in the Angels: one would safeguard himself from believing in superstitions and fables.

Merits of belief in the Angels: one would recognize the mercy Allah shows to his slaves; for Allah assigned to every individual angels who guard him and take care of his affairs.

MERITS OF BELIEF IN THE ANGELS

1. One would understand the greatness of Allah, His power and ability, and His All-Encompassing Knowledge, from the greatness of His creation, which is a proof confirming the greatness of the Creator.
2. When a Muslim knows that there are Angels who record all that he says and does, and that everything he does is either for him or held against him, he would be keen to perform righteous deeds and abstain from sins, whether he is alone or in public.
3. One would safeguard himself from believing in superstitions and fables.
4. One would recognize the mercy Allah shows to His slaves; for Allah assigned to every individual angels who guard him and take care of his affairs.

---

(1) Angels who preserve the deeds of men in records

23 | BELIEF IN THE ANGELS

MY FIRST STEPS IN ISLAM

BELIEF IN THE BOOKS OF ALLAH

One must believe that Allah revealed Heavenly Books to His Messengers in order to convey them to mankind. These Books, during their times, contained nothing but the truth. All these Books call people to worship Allah alone, and that He is the Creator, Proprietor and Owner, and to Him belong the beautiful Attributes and Names.

Allah says:

"Indeed We have sent Our Messengers with clear proofs, and revealed with them the Scripture and the Balance that mankind may maintain [their affairs] in justice." [57:25]

SOME OF THE BOOKS ARE:

1. The Scriptures of Ibraheem (Abraham) and Musa (Moses):
The Qur'an has given a brief insight about the religious fundamentals found in these scriptures. Allah says:
"Or, has he not been informed of what is in the scriptures of Musa? And (of) Ibraheem, who fulfilled [the commandments]: That no bearer of burden shall bear the burden of another; and that man shall have nothing but what he strives for; and that his striving shall soon be seen. Then shall he be rewarded for it with the fullest reward; and that to your Lord is the goal." [53:36-42]

2. The Torah: The Torah is the Sacred Book which was revealed to Musa. Allah says:
"Verily, We sent down the Torah, in which was guidance and light. The prophets who submitted [to Allah] judged by

A Muslim must believe in all the Heavenly Books and he must believe that they are from Allah. It is not lawful for him to abide by their laws though, since these Books were revealed to certain nations at certain times.

it for the Jews, as did the rabbis and scholars by that with which they were entrusted of the Scripture of Allah, and they were witnesses thereto. So do not fear the people but fear Me, and do not exchange My verses for a small price. And whoever does not judge by what Allah has revealed - then it is those who are the disbelievers." [5:44]

3. **THE ZABOOR (PSALMS):** The Zaboor is the Book which was revealed to Dawood (David). Allah says:

"…and to Dawood We gave the Zaboor." [4:163]

4. **The Injeel (Gospel):** The Injeel is the Book which was revealed to 'Eesaa (Jesus). Allah says:

"And We sent, following in their footsteps, Jesus, the son of Mary, confirming that which came before him in the Torah; and We gave him the Gospel, in which was guidance and light and confirming that which preceded it of the Torah as guidance and instruction for the righteous." [5:46]

A Muslim must believe in all the Heavenly Books and he must believe that they are from Allah. It is not lawful for him to abide by their laws though, since these Books were revealed to certain nations at certain times.

The Qur'an has explained some of what was found in the Torah and the Injeel; such as the prophecy of Muhammad ﷺ:

"…but My mercy encompasses all things. So I will decree it [especially] for those who fear Me and give zakah and those who believe in Our verses. Those who follow the Messenger, the unlettered prophet, whom they find written in what they have of the Torah and the Gospel, who enjoins upon them what is right and forbids them what is wrong and makes lawful for them the good things and prohibits for them the evil and relieves them of their burden and the shackles which were upon them. So they who have believed in him, honored him, supported him and followed the light which was sent down with him - it is those who will be the successful." [7:156-157]

5. **The Noble Qur'an:** One must hold the following beliefs concerning it:

A. One must believe that the Qur'an is the Speech of Allah which Jibreel (Gabriel) brought to Muhammad ﷺ in a clear Arabic language. Allah says:

"The Trustworthy Spirit has brought it down, Upon your heart, [O Muhammad] - that you may be of the warners - In a clear Arabic language." [26:193-195]

B. One must believe that the Qur'an is the last of the Heavenly Books, which confirms the previous Books concerning the Message of Tawheed and the obligation to worship and obey Him. All previous Books were abrogated by the Qur'an. Allah says:

"[It is] He has sent down upon you, [O Muhammad], the Book in truth, confirming what was before it. And He revealed the Torah and the Gospel. Before, as guidance for the people. And He revealed the Qur'an. Indeed, those who disbelieve in the verses of Allah will have a severe punishment, and Allah is exalted in Might, the Owner of Retribution." [3:3-4]

C. One must believe that the Qur'an contains all divine laws. Allah says:

"This day, I have perfected your religion for you, completed My Favor upon you, and have chosen for you Islam as a religion." [5:3]

D. One must believe that it was revealed to mankind at large; not to a specific nation, as were previously revealed Heavenly Books. Allah says:

"And We have not sent you except comprehensively to mankind as a bringer of good tidings and a warner. But most of the people do not know." [34:28]

E. One must believe that Allah has preserved the Qur'an from all distortions, adulterations, additions, or impairments. Allah says:

"Indeed, We have sent down the revelation and surely, We shall guard it [from distortion]." [15:9]

One must believe that the Qur'an contains all Divine laws.

One must believe that the Qur'an is the last of the Heavenly Books, which confirms the previous Books concerning the Message of Tawheed and the obligation to worship and obey Him.

THE MERITS OF BELIEF IN Allah'S BOOKS

1. One would realize the mercy and love Allah has for His servants; since He revealed to them Books which guide them to the path which leads to His pleasure. He safeguarded man from confusion and from the evil of Shaytaan[1].

2. One would realize the great wisdom of Allah; since He gave each nation a set of laws that suited them during their times.

3. To distinguish true believers from those who are not. It is incumbent upon one who believes in his own Book to believe in the other Heavenly Books.

4. To increase the good deeds of the believers; for the one who believes in his Book and the Books that came after his Book, would receive his reward twice. Allah says: "Those to whom We gave the Scripture before it - they are believers in it. And when it is recited to them, they say: 'We believe in it. Verily, it is the truth from our Lord. Indeed even before it we have been from those who submit themselves to Allah. These will be given their reward twice over, because they are patient, and repel evil with good, and spend (in charity) out of what We have provided them." [28:52-54]

QUR'AN

---

(1) Shaytaan: Satan: A Jinn named Iblees who disobeyed Allah's order to prostrate to Adam, and therefore was cursed for eternity. He asked Allah for respite, which He in turn granted, to strive to lead humanity to the Hellfire with him.

MY FIRST STEPS IN ISLAM

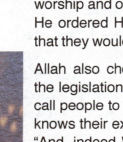

BELIEF IN ALLAH'S MESSENGERS

04

The merits of belief in the messengers: one would realize the mercy and love Allah has for His servants; since he sent to them messengers who conveyed to them his religion. They in themselves were examples whom people emulated.

It is to believe that Allah chose the finest amongst mankind to be Messengers whom He sent to His creation with specific legislations; to worship and obey Allah, and to establish His Deen and His Tawheed. He ordered His Messengers to convey the Message to people, so that they would not have any proof against Allah[1] after He sent them.

Allah also chose people amongst mankind as Prophets to affirm the legislation and Deen of the messenger sent before them and to call people to it. There are many prophets and messengers; no one knows their exact number except Allah. Allah says:

"And, indeed We have sent Messengers before you [O Muhammad ﷺ]; of some of them We have related to you their story, and of some We have not related to you their story. And it was not for any messenger to bring a sign [or verse] except by permission of Allah." [40:78]

One must believe in all of them and that they were human; they were not supernatural beings. Allah says:

"And We sent not before you [O Muhammad ﷺ] but men to whom We inspired, so ask the people of the message if you do not know. And We did not create them with bodies that had no need to eat food, nor were they immortal." [21:7-8]

Allah says about Jesus in the Qur'an:

"The Messiah, son of Mary, was not but a messenger; [other] messengers have passed on before him. And his mother was a supporter of truth. They both used to eat food. Look how We make clear to them the signs; then look how they are deluded." [5:75]

One must believe in all of them. If one believes in some and disbelieves in others, he leaves the folds of Islam. Allah says:

"Verily, those who disbelieve in Allah and His Messengers and wish

---

(1) They will not be able to say, "Had Allah sent us messengers, we would have followed His commands and become of the believers."

to make distinction between Allah and His Messengers saying, 'We believe in some but reject others', and wish to adopt a way in between. They are in truth disbelievers. And We have prepared for the disbelievers a humiliating torment." [4:150-151]

The first messenger was Noah, and the last was Muhammad ﷺ.

WHO IS MUHAMMAD ﷺ?

MUHAMMAD ﷺ

His name is Muhammad bin[2] Abdullah bin Abdul-Muttalib bin Haashim. His Kunyah[3] is Abul-Qaasim. He was from the Arab tribe of Quraish whose ancestry traces back to 'Adnaan. 'Adnaan was from the children of Ismaa`eel, the Prophet of Allah and son of Ibraheem, the Khaleel[4] of Allah.

The Prophet ﷺ said:
"Indeed Allah chose the tribe of Kinaanah over other tribes from the children of Ismaa'eel. He chose the Quraish over other tribes of Kinaanah. He chose Banu Haashim over the other families of the Quraish. And He chose me from Banu Haashim." (Muslim #2276)

He received his first revelation from Allah at the age of forty, and he remained in Makkah thereafter for thirteen years calling to the Tawheed of Allah. He then migrated to Madinah and called its people to Islam, and they accepted it. There, Allah revealed the remaining legislations. He conquered Makkah eight years after his migration, and he died when he was sixty-three, after Allah revealed to him the whole Qur'an. All the legislations of the religion were revealed, completed and perfected, and all the whole of the Arabian peninsula had accepted Islam.

THE MERITS OF BELIEF IN THE MESSENGERS

1. One would realize the mercy and love Allah has for His servants; since He sent to them Messengers who conveyed to them His religion. They in themselves were examples whom people emulated.

2. To distinguish the believers who are truthful in their Faith from others; for it is incumbent upon one who believes in his own Messenger to believe in other Messengers who are mentioned in his Book.

3. Those of the people of the Book (Jews and Christians) who believe in their Messengers and then believe in Muhammad, may Allah exalt his mention, would receive double reward.

---

(2) Bin, pl. Banu: 'the Son of…', "the children of…"
(3) Kunyah: A name similar to a Nickname.
(4) Khaleel: the one whom Allah loves most.

MY FIRST STEPS IN ISLAM

05 BELIEF IN THE LAST DAY

It is to believe that the life of this world will come to an end. Allah says:

"Whatsoever is on the earth will perish." [55:26]

1. To believe in the life of the Barzakh: This life is the time after one's death until the Last Day. In it, the believer will live a life of pleasure, while the disbeliever will be punished. Allah says:

"The Fire; they are exposed to it, morning and afternoon, And the Day the Hour appears [it will be said], 'Make the people of Pharaoh enter the severest punishment.'" [40:46]

2. To believe in the Resurrection: Allah will resurrect mankind, naked, barefooted, and uncircumcised. Allah says:

"The disbelievers claim that they will never be resurrected. Say, 'Yes, by my Lord, you will surely be resurrected; then you will surely be informed of what you did. And that, for Allah, is easy.'" [64:7]

Belief in the last day: to believe in the resurrection: Allah will resurrect mankind, naked, barefooted, and uncircumcised.

3. To believe in the Gathering: Allah will gather all creation together and call them to account. Allah says:

"And [warn of] the Day when We will remove the mountains and you will see the earth prominent, and We will gather them and not leave behind from them anyone." [18:47]

4. To believe that people will be brought before Allah in rows: Allah says:

"And they shall be brought before your Lord, standing in rows: 'You have certainly come to Us just as We created you the first time. But you claimed that We would never make for you an appointment.'" [18:48]

5. To believe that one's limbs will bear witness. Allah says:
"Till, when they reach it, their hearing and their eyes, and their skins will testify against them as to what they used to do. And they will say to their skins, 'Why do you testify against us?' They will say: 'Allah has caused us to speak, He causes all things to speak: and He created you the first time, and to Him you are made to return.' And you have not been hiding yourselves, lest your ears, and your eyes, and your skins testify against you; but you thought that Allah knew not much of what you were doing." [41:20-22]

6. To believe in the Questioning. Allah says:
"But stop them; verily they are to be questioned. [They will be asked], 'What is [wrong] with you? Why do you not help each other?' But they, that Day, are in surrender." [37:24-26]

7. To believe in the Siraat (Bridge over the Hellfire) and that everyone must pass over it. Allah says:
"There is not one of you but will pass over [Hell]; this is upon your Lord an inevitability decreed." [19:71]

8. To believe in the weighing of deeds. Allah will call people to account and reward those who did well with what they deserve, due to their righteous deeds, their faith, and adherence to their Messengers, and He will punish those who did evil. Allah says:
"And We place the scales of justice for the Day of Resurrection, so no soul will be treated unjustly at all. And if there is [even] the weight of a mustard seed, We will bring it forth. And sufficient are We as accountant." [21:47]

9. To believe in the handing out of Scrolls and Books. Allah says:
"Then, as for him who will be given his Record in his right hand, He surely will receive an easy reckoning. And he will return to his family in joy! But

MY FIRST STEPS IN ISLAM

whosoever is given his Record behind his back. He will cry out for destruction. And [enter to] burn in a Blaze." [84:7-12]

10. To believe that people will be rewarded with Jannah or Hellfire in an everlasting and eternal life that will never end. Allah says:

"Verily, they who disbelieved among the People of the Scripture and the polytheists will be in the fire of Hell, abiding eternally therein. Those are the worst of creatures. Verily, those who believe and do righteous deeds, they are the best of creatures. Their reward with Allah will be gardens of perpetual residence beneath which rivers flow, wherein they will abide forever, Allah being pleased with them and they with Him. That is for whoever has feared his Lord." [98:6-8]

11. To believe in the Hawd[(1)], Intercession, and all other things which the Messenger of Allah ﷺ informed us.

Belief in the last day. To believe in the Gathering: Allah will gather all creation together and call them to account.

Belief in the last day: To believe that people will be rewarded with Jannah or Hellfire in an everlasting and eternal life that will never end.

THE MERITS OF BELIEF IN THE LAST DAY:

1. It would make one prepare himself for that Day, by performing good deeds, and competing therein, and abstaining from sinful acts and fearing His punishment.

2. It would comfort the believers; since they know what they missed in this world, Allah would reward them with better in the Hereafter.

3. To distinguish the believers who are truthful in their faith from those who are not.

"Whatsoever is on the earth will perish." [55:26]

---

(1) The pool which Allah granted the Prophet ﷺ; whoever drinks from it once, will never feel thirsty thereafter.

اليوم الآخر
THE LAST DAY

MY FIRST STEPS IN ISLAM

06 BELIEF IN QADAA' AND QADAR[1]

It is to believe that Allah knew everything before it came into being, and what will happen to it afterward. He then brought them into existence, all in accordance to His perfect knowledge and measure. Allah says:

"Verily, We have created all things with Qadar." [54:49]

Everything which occurred in the past, that which is occurring in the present and what will occur in the future is known to Allah before it came into existence. Allah then brought it into being, all in accordance to His Will and Measure. The Messenger of Allah ﷺ said:

"A person is not a Muslim until he believes in Qadar, its good and its evil consequences - until he knows that whatever happened to him would have never missed him, and what did not happen to him would never have occurred." [Tirmidhi]

Everything which occurred in the past, that which is occurring in the present and what will occur in the future is known to Allah before it came into existence.

This belief does not contradict the fact that one must strive to attain things. To clarify this, if a person wants a child he must do certain things to achieve this goal; such as getting married. After he does all that is in his power, he may be granted what he wishes or not. The reason for this, is that a person would realize that what he does to achieve his goal is not in fact the true cause behind it; rather it is the Will of Allah. These 'means' to fulfill our goals are also considered from the Qadar of Allah. The Prophet ﷺ was asked:

"O Messenger of Allah, do the verses and supplications we

---

(1) Qadaa´ and Qadar: These two Arabic words are usually translated as 'fate', 'destiny', or 'pre-ordainment'. Many of these English words lead people to incorrectly believe this concept, so it is best to leave them as Arabic terms and understand them in their true light.

recite and the medicine we take to cure ourselves waive the Qadar of Allah?" He replied, "They are themselves from the Qadar of Allah." [Mustadrak al-Haakim]

Hunger, thirst, feeling cold, are from the Qadaa' and Qadr. One seeks to satisfy hunger through eating, thirst through drinking and coldness by keeping warm. A person seeks to fend themselves from what was decreed for them from hunger, thirst and coldness by what was decreed for them from eating, drinking, and seeking warmth. They seek to prevent one Qadar with another.

One must, fulfill whatever means are possible to achieve his goal, for the means are also a part of Qadaa' and Qadr. One becomes pleased with the results (whatever they may be), which in turn produces peace of heart and spiritual comfort. There is no room for stress, worry, or sadness. It is known that stress and unrest of heart leads to many sicknesses. Having belief in this concept prevents and cures many of these sicknesses. Allah says:
"No evil befalls on the earth nor in your own souls, but it is in a book before We bring it into existence; surely that is easy for Allah: So that you may not grieve for what has escaped you, nor be exultant at what He has given you; and Allah does not love any arrogant boaster." [57:22-23]

It encourages knowledge and exploration of what Allah created in this universe. Afflictions, such as disease, drive humans to seek their cure, and this is done by searching for the sources of medicine which Allah, the Exalted, created in this universe.

It eases the effects of calamities faced by humans and eliminates the feeling of regret about what has already passed. If someone loses money in a business, this is considered a hardship. If this hardship was followed by the feeling of remorse and sorrow, it would result in two hardships: the hardship of the financial loss and the hardship of feeling remorse and sorrow. If one believes in the Divine Measure of Qadaa' and Qadr, he would be pleased with what has occurred, because he knows that it was inevitable. The Prophet ﷺ said:
"Be keen to do what benefits you and seek help in Allah, and do not be neglectful in doing so. And if any mishap befalls you, do not say, 'If only I had only done such and such,' but rather say, 'This is the Qadar of Allah, and whatever He Wills He does', for indeed (the saying of) 'if' opens the door for the Devil." [Muslim]

It increases one's dependence upon Allah and removes fear of the creation. Ibn 'Abbaas said

"I was behind the Messenger of Allah ﷺ one day and he ﷺ said to me:

'O young boy, I will teach you some words: Guard Allah's commandments and he will guard you. Guard Allah's commandments, you will find Him in front of you. And If you ask, then ask Allah, and if you seek help, then seek help in Allah and know that if the whole world was to gather to help you, they would never be able to help you except with something which Allah has already written for you. If the whole world was to gather to bring you some harm, they would not be able to harm you except with something which Allah has already written for you. The pens have been lifted, and the scrolls have dried.'" [Tirmidhi]

The merits of belief in qadaa´ and qadar: one strengthens his dependence upon Allah (in achieving results) after fulfilling their means.

Belief in Qadar is not, as some mistakenly think, a call to put one's trust in Allah without striving or fulfilling the means, for the Messenger of Allah ﷺ replied to a person who asked him:
"Should I leave my camel untied and trust in Allah (that it will be here when I get back)?" He said, "Tie it, and then put your trust in Allah." [Ibn Hibbaan]

He also said:
"By Him in Whose Hands is my soul, that one of you goes and chops wood, ties it, and carries it on his back is better than for him to go and beg people, whether they give him money or not." [Bukhari]

The merits of belief in qadaa´ and qadar: one becomes pleased with whatever results are realized, which in turn produces peace of heart and spiritual comfort.

1. One strengthens his dependence upon Allah (in achieving results) after fulfilling their means.
2. One becomes pleased with whatever results are realized, which in turn produces peace of heart and spiritual comfort. Allah says:
"No disaster strikes upon the earth or among yourselves except that it is in a register before We bring it into being - indeed that, for Allah, is easy. So that you may not grieve for what has escaped you, nor be exultant at what He has given you; and Allah does not love any arrogant boaster." [57:22-23]
3. It eases the effects of calamities. The Prophet ﷺ said:
"The strong believer is better and more beloved to Allah than a weak believer, and in each one there is good. Be keen to do what benefits you and seek Allah's help, and do not be neglectful in doing so. And if any mishap befalls you, do not say, 'If only I had only done such and such,' but rather say, 'This is the Qadar of Allah, and whatever He Wills He does (*Qadarullaah wa maa shaa fa'al*),' for indeed, 'if,' opens the door for the Devil." (Muslim #2664)
4. It increases one's reward and effaces his sins. The Prophet ﷺ said:
"No Muslims is fatigued, is stricken with illness, feels stress, worry, sadness, or harm, not even a thorn which pricks him, except that Allah forgives sins through it." (Bukhari #5318)

WHAT ONE SHOULD DO AFTER PRONOUNCING THE SHAHAADATAYN

The Intention (Niyyah). One must intend (in his heart) that he is performing ghusl to purify himself from a state of major impurity - whether janâbah, menstruation or postpartum bleeding.

After pronouncing the Shahaadatayn, it is from the Sunnah that a person does the following:

1. It is recommended that a person takes a complete bath (ghusl) with pure water and then perform a two-unit prayer. It is narrated that Thumamah al-Hanafi was taken captive and the Prophet ﷺ would keep coming to him and say: "What do you say, O Thumamah?" He would reply, "If you decide to kill me, you would be justified because I have killed; if you let me free, you would be letting free one who shows gratitude; and if you desire wealth, we will give you what you please." The Companions of the Prophet ﷺ liked to ransom captives, and so they said, "What would we gain if we killed him?" So finally one day, the Prophet ﷺ decided to set [Thumamah] free, and he thereafter accepted Islam. The Prophet ﷺ sent him to the walled garden of Abu Talhah, commanding him to take a complete bath (ghusl). He performed a complete bath and prayed a two unit prayer, and the Prophet ﷺ said, "Your brother's Islam is sincere." (Saheeh ibn Khuzaimah #253)

HOW TO PERFORM A COMPLETE BATH (GHUSL)

The Intention (Niyyah). One must intend (in his heart) that he is performing ghusl to purify himself from a state of major impurity[1] - whether janâbah, menstruation or postpartum bleeding - without uttering such intention verbally.

- Say "Bismillah" ("I begin with the name of Allah").
- Wash the hands and then the private parts.
- Next, perform wudhu[2] as you would for the prayer. You may delay washing of the feet until the end of the ghusl.
- You should pour [at least] three handfuls of water on your head, running the fingers through the hair so that water reaches the roots of his hair and scalp.
- Then pour water over the rest of the body, beginning with the right side. You should make sure to wash the armpits, ears, navel, and the creases of the skin if fat, for these creases prevent water from reaching the areas of skin concealed within. You should then wash the feet if not already done while making wudhu [before performing the ghusl]. 'Aa`ishah reported:

"When Allah's Messenger ﷺ would perform ghusl due to sexual intercourse, he would first wash his hands, then pour water with his right hand into his left, washing his private parts. After that he would perform wudhu as he would for the prayer, and then take water and rub it into the roots of his hair with his fingers. [Lastly] he would wash his feet." (Muslim #316)

Ghusl becomes obligatory after one of the following things:

1. Ejaculation of semen due to desire, nocturnal emission, or the like.

2. Sexual intercourse, even if it does not result in ejaculation.

3. Following menstruation,

4. Following postpartum bleeding.

WUDHU

One should perform wudhu before the prayer, for the Prophet ﷺ said:
"Prayer is not accepted without purification...." (Muslim #224)

---

(1) There are two types of impurity, major and minor, both will be explained later.

(2) Wudhu is washing specific parts of the body, in a specific sequence, to remove oneself from a state of minor impurity. It will be explained in detail.

MY FIRST STEPS IN ISLAM

Allah says:
"O you who have believed, when you rise to [perform] prayer, wash your faces and your forearms to the elbows and wipe over your heads and wash your feet to the ankles..." [5:6]

One should perform wudhu in the following manner:
Humraan the freed slave of 'Uthmaan bin Affaan said:
"I saw 'Uthmaan perform wudhu. He poured water on his hands thrice, then he rinsed his mouth and nose, washed his face thrice, washed his right hand up to his elbow thrice, washed his left hand up to his elbow thrice, wiped over his head once, washed his right foot thrice, and then his left foot thrice. He then said, 'I saw the Messenger of Allah ﷺ perform wudhu like this', and he said: 'Whoever performs wudhu like my wudhu, and then prays two Rakaat not thinking about anything else, Allah will forgive him all his previous sins.'" (Bukhari #1832)

One should not delay washing one part of the body so that the previously washed part becomes dry.

One should wash the parts of wudhu in the correct sequence. He should not contradict the sequence mentioned in the verse, for Allah mentioned the obligatory acts of wudhu in a specific sequence.

1. One should intend that he is performing wudhu to purify himself from a minor state of impurity. The proof that intention (niyyah) is obligatory as seen from the statement of the Prophet ﷺ:

"All deeds are considered by their intentions, and each person will be rewarded according to what he intends…" (Bukhari #1 & Muslim #45)

2. One should say, "Bismillaah," before making wudhu. The Prophet ﷺ said:

"There is no Prayer for one who does not perform wudhu, and there is no wudhu for one who does not mention the name of Allah." (Abu Dawood #101 & ibn Maajah # 399)

3. One should wash his hands thrice at the beginning of the wudhu.

4. One should rinse his mouth and clean his nose by sniffing water into it thrice. He should blow the water out of his nose using the left hand.

5. One should wash his face thrice. The face consists of the area starting from the hairline at the top of the forehead to the bottom of the chin or beard, vertically, and from right ear to the left, horizontally.

6. One should wash his hands from the tips of fingers to the elbow (including the elbow itself) beginning first with the right hand, then the left. If he is wearing a ring or a watch, he must remove it in order to allow the water to reach the skin underneath it.

7. One must wipe over his head once. This is done by wetting the hands and passing them over the head, beginning from the front, proceeding to the back, and then passing them back over the head to the front. Abdullah b. Zaid narrated:

"Allah's Messenger ﷺ passed his hands over his head starting from the front, proceeding to the back. He started from his forehead and passed them over to the top of his neck, and then passed them back to the place where he started from." (Bukhari #183 & Muslim#235)

8. One should wipe his ears by inserting wet index fingers in the cavity of the ears, and wipe the back part of the ears with the thumbs. Ibn Abbas described the wudhu of the Prophet ﷺ saying:

"He then wiped over his head and put his index fingers into his ears. He wiped the backside of his ears with his thumbs, and the insides of his ear with his index fingers." (Abu Dawud #123)

9. One should wash his feet three times from the tips of the toes up to and including the ankles. Abu Hurairah said that the Messenger of Allah ﷺ saw a person who did not wash his heels, and he said to him:

"Woe to the heels from the Hellfire!" (Bukhari#60 & Muslim #142)

10. One should wash the parts of wudhu in the correct sequence. He should not contradict the sequence mentioned in the verse, for Allah mentioned the obligatory acts of wudhu in a specific sequence.

11. One should not delay washing one part of the body so that the previously washed part becomes dry.

MY FIRST STEPS IN ISLAM

It is mentioned in a Hadeeth that the Prophet ﷺ saw a man praying, but a portion of his foot - the size of a coin - was not wet. Upon this, the Prophet ﷺ ordered him to repeat his wudhu and prayer.[3] (Abu Dâwud #175)

One must remove anything from the parts that must be washed in the wudhu which might prevent water from reaching the skin underneath it, such as nail-polish, and similar things.

One remains in a state of wudhu unless something invalidates it, such as urination, defecation, passing of gas, pre-seminal fluid, prostatic fluid, false menstruation (vaginal bleeding other than menses) eating camel meat, touching the private parts with one's hand directly, and deep sleep.

TAYAMMUM (DRY ABLUTION)

If there is no water available to perform wudhu or ghusl, or there is a factor present which prevents the use of water, such as illness, or the inability to use water, it is lawful to perform Tayammum.

Tayammum takes the place of water in purifying oneself from states of impurity, and it is performed as follows:

1. One should strike the ground once with his hands while his fingers are spread apart,

2. One should then wipe over his face once with his palms,

3. One should wipe both hands until his wrists.

THE PRAYER

It is obligatory upon you to establish the prayer (Salaah) for it is the backbone of the religion; without it, one's Islam would not be complete. The Prophet ﷺ said [striking an example between the religion and a camel]:

---

(3) Note that he did not merely order him to wash his foot, but rather he ordered him to repeat the entire wudhu' as well as his prayer.

One must remove anything from the parts that must be washed in the wudhu which might prevent water from reaching the skin underneath it.

The Salaah establishes a relationship between the slave and Allah. He enters a private conversation with Him, supplicating Him in sincere humbleness.

"The first matter that the slave will be brought to account for on the Day of Judgment is the prayer. If it is sound, then the rest of his deeds will be sound. And if it is deficient, then the rest of his deeds will be deficient." (Tabarani, Saheeh al-Jaam'i)

Salaah is a term which denotes a group of words and actions which start with takbeer, saying, "Allahu Akbar" (which means "Allah is Greater"), and ending with tasleem, saying, "As-Salaamu 'alaykum wa Rahmatullaah" (which means "May the Peace and Mercy of Allah be upon you").

THE REWARD OF SALAAH

When one establishes the Salaah, he benefits in the following ways:

1. Spiritual joy: The Salaah establishes a relationship between the slave and Allah. He enters a private conversation with Him, supplicating Him in sincere humbleness.

2. Peace of heart and tranquility. The Prophet ﷺ said:
"Women and perfume have been made beloved to me, and the Salaah has been made the delight of my eyes." (Nasa'ie #3940)

3. The Salaah prevents one from all sinful and immoral deeds. Allah says:
"Indeed, prayer prohibits immorality and wrongdoing, and the remembrance of Allah is greater. And Allah knows that which you do." [29:45]

4. The Salaah strengthens the bonds of love and unity among the Muslims. It breaks down all social differences that may exist between them; they all stand together side by side in rows, the old and young, the rich and poor, the noble and ignoble. All people are the same, humbling themselves before Allah, facing the same direction (the Qiblah[(4)]) performing the same actions, reciting the same recitation, all at the same time.

PRAYER TIMES

There are five prayers during the day and night which are obligatory upon every Muslim. All men should establish Salaah in congregation (jamaa'ah) in the Masjid, unless they have a valid excuse; while women earn a greater reward when they pray in their homes; though they are allowed to pray in the masjid as well.

The Messenger of Allah ﷺ was asked about the times of prayers. He said:
"The time for the morning prayer (lasts) as long as the first visible part of the

---

(4) Qiblah: the direction of the Ka'bah.

rising sun does not appear. And the time of the noon prayer is when the sun declines from the zenith, and the time for the afternoon prayer has not yet entered. And the time of the afternoon prayer prayer is so long as the sun does not become pale and its first visible part does not set. And the time for the evening prayer is when the sun disappears and (it lasts) till the twilight is no more. And the (preferred) time for the night prayer is up to the midnight." (Muslim #612)

PRAYER CHART

There are five prayers during the day and night which are obligatory upon every Muslim. All men should establish Salaah in congregation (jamaa'ah) in the Masjid, unless they have a valid excuse.

Name & Type of Recitation	# of Rak'ahs	Its Time	# of Sunnah Prayers
Dhuhr (Noon) Silent	4	It **starts** from the time the sun starts to descend towards the west after its zenith, and **ends** when the length of an object's shadow is equal to the actual object's height.	4 rak'ahs before and 2 rak'ahs after.
'Asr (Afternoon) Silent	4	It **starts** when the time of Dhuhr ends, and **ends** when the sun sets.	None
Maghrib (Dusk) Audible	3	It **starts** when the Sun has totally set, and **ends** when the red color of dusk disappears.	2 rak'ahs after
'Ishaa' (Night) Audible	4	It **starts** when the time of Maghrib ends, and **ends** at the first appearance of light before dawn.	2 rak'ahs after
Fajr (Dawn) Audible	2	It **starts** at the first appearance of light at dawn, and **ends** when the sun starts to rise.	2 rak'ahs before

THE PRE-REQUISITES OF SALAAH

Know that the Salaah has certain prerequisites; if one leaves them, his prayer is invalid. They are as follows:

1. Praying them in their proper times.

2. One must purify himself from minor and major impurities. Allah, the Exalted, says: "O you who have believed, when you rise to [perform] prayer, wash your faces and your forearms to the elbows and wipe over your heads and wash your feet to the ankles. And if you are in a state of janabah[(1)], then purify yourselves." [5:6]

3. One's body must be clean from any impurities. The Prophet ﷺ said: "Be careful to keep yourself clean from urine, for indeed, the majority of the punishment of the grave is due to people not doing so." (Haakim #654 and verified)

One must keep his clothes pure from any impurities. Allah says: "And your clothing purify." [74:4]

One must make sure that the place he is praying in is free from impurities. A

---

(1) Major impurity

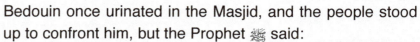

MY FIRST STEPS IN ISLAM

Bedouin once urinated in the Masjid, and the people stood up to confront him, but the Prophet ﷺ said:

"Leave him and pour a bucket of water where he urinated, for you have been sent to make things easy, not to make things hard." (Bukhari #217)

4. Covering one's 'awrah[(2)]. For a man, it is the area between the navel and the knees, but in salaah, it includes both his shoulders. As for a woman, it is her whole body, but in salaah, she does not need to cover her face and hands. Allah says:
"O Children of Adam! Take your adornment at every masjid..." [7:31]

5. One must face the Qiblah. Allah says:
"So turn your face to the direction of al-Masjid al-Haraam. And wherever you [believers] are, turn your faces toward it [in prayer]." [2:144]

A woman in her menstrual period, or postpartum bleeding should not pray until her bleeding stops. Thereupon, she should perform a complete bath (ghusl) and resume praying, and perform ablution (wudhu) for each prayer if she invalidates it. She should not make up any prayers she missed while bleeding.

HOW TO PERFORM SALAAH

1. One should make wudhu by using pure water, as Allah ﷻ orders:
"O you who have believed, when you rise to [perform] prayer, wash your faces and your forearms to the elbows and wipe over your heads and wash your feet to the ankles. And if you are in a state of janabah, then purify yourselves." [5:6]

2. One must face the Qiblah, which is the direction of the Ka'bah, with his whole body and intend (with his heart) the specific prayer he is performing, without speaking it verbally.

---

(2) 'Awrah: The parts of the body which are forbidden for another to look at.

AFTER PRONOUNCING THE SHAHADATAAN

3. One must pronounce Takbeerat-ul-Ihraam[3] by saying, "Allahu Akbar". He should do so while looking at the place he will prostrate in, raising his hands to the level of his shoulders or his earlobes, extending his fingers [with his palms] facing the Qiblah.

4. One should put his hands on his chest, placing his right hand over his left, and can recite the opening supplication (Du'aa-ul-Istiftaah), but this is supplication is not mandatory:

"Subhaanak-Allahumma wa bi hamdika, wa tabaarak-Asmuka, wa ta'aala jaddukka wa laa ilaaha ghayruka."

Meaning: Far removed are You from every imperfection, O Allah, and all praise belongs to You. Blessed is Your Name. Great and Exalted is Your Kingdom. None has the right to be worshipped except You."

One should then say:

"A'oodhu billaahi min ash-Shaytaan ir-Rajeem. Bismillaah ir-Rahmaan ir-Raheem."

Meaning: I seek refuge with Allah from Satan, the Rejected One. I begin with the Name of Allah, the Most Merciful, and the Bestower of Mercy.

Then one should recite Surah al-Faatihah, saying 'Ameen' after finishing it; saying it aloud in the prayers in which he reads aloud and silently in the silent prayers. After this, one should recite whatever he wishes from the Qur'an.

5. After completing recitation, one should bow (rukoo') by bending the back forward. First he should say:

"Allahu Akbar."

Meaning: Allah is Greater.

He should raise his hands to his shoulders or earlobes while doing so. Then he should make rukoo' (bowing posture) extending his back, making his head level with it. At this point he should place his hands with his fingers spread on his knees, keeping the elbows away from his sides. In the rukoo', one should say three times:

---

(3) Takbir means to say Allahu Akbar or God is Greater. Ihram literally means to enter into a physical state in which certain actions are not permissible.

As for Takbiratul Ihram, it means that we are saying Allahu Akbar to indicate the start of a period where all permissible things are no longer permissible to us except those which are allowed in prayer. In other words, the moment we say Allahu Akbar and we raise our hands, we forbid ourselves from all the general permissible things. We cannot eat, sleep, drink, laugh, talk, jump, move about unnecessarily, etc.

MY FIRST STEPS IN ISLAM

"Subhaana Rub-biyal-Adheem."
Meaning: Far removed is my Lord, the Most Magnificent, from every imperfection.

6. One should raise his head [and upper body] from the rukoo, and raise his hands to his shoulders or earlobes, saying:
"Sami'allahu liman Hamidah."
Meaning: Allah answers the supplication of those who praise and extol Him.

One should say this whether he is praying alone or leading others in Prayer. After fully returning to a standing position, one should say:
"Rabanaa wa lak-al-Hamd."
Meaning: Our Lord, and to You belongs all praise.

7. Next, one must prostrate (Sujood) and say:
"Allahu Akbar."
Meaning: Allah is Greater.

He should not raise his hands to his shoulders or ears in this case. He should descend, placing his knees on the ground before his hands - if it is not hard for him - and prostrate on seven parts: his face (forehead and nose), his hands, his knees, and the feet. The fingers and toes should face the Qiblah, and his fingers should be drawn together (not spread apart). He should keep his elbows away from his sides and his knees away from his stomach and his thighs away from his legs. He should lift his elbows and forearms off the ground and say (three times):
"Subhaana Rub-biyal-A'laa."
Meaning: Far removed is my Lord, the Most High, from every imperfection.

One should supplicate[4] as much as possible in the sujood, for the Prophet ﷺ said:
"As for the rukoo', aggrandize the Lord and as for the sujood, make as much supplication as you can, for [it is the place where] it is most likely to be accepted." (Muslim #479)

---

(4) He may supplicate Allah in his own words, or native language.

8. One should raise his head from the sujood and say, "Allahu Akbar." One should not raise his hands to his shoulders or earlobes while saying so. He should lay his left foot flat on the ground [pointing to the right] and sit upon it, and prop his right foot upright [with the bottom of his toes on the ground facing the Qiblah]. One should place his hands on his thighs and knees, and then say thrice: "Rabbighfir li."

Meaning: My Lord, forgive me.

In addition to this, he may say:
"Allahumm-aghfir li, warhamni, wahdini, warzuqni, wa 'aafini, wajburni."

Meaning: O Allah, forgive me, have mercy upon me, guide me, grant me sustenance, keep me in a state of safety and well-being, and strengthen my weakness.

9. One has to perform a second sujood saying, "Allahu Akbar," without raising his hands. He should do as he did in the first sujood.

10. Then one raises his head from sujood saying, "Allahu Akbar," without raising his hands to his shoulders or earlobes. Next, he should stand up and perform the second Rak'ah, supporting himself with his knees, if possible. If this is difficult, then he may stand up while supporting himself with his hands.

After standing, he should recite Surah al-Faatihah again and whatever he wishes to recite from the Qur'an, just as he did in the first rak'ah.

11. If one is performing a prayer which consists of two Rak'aat, such as Fajr, Jumu'ah, or 'Eid, after the second prostration he should sit with his right foot propped up, sitting on his left foot laid flat [pointing to the right]. He should clench his right hand and place it on the lower part of his right thigh, and he should point with his finger during his supplication and mentioning Allah (the tashahhud) symbolizing His Tawheed. He should place his left hand on the bottom, front part of his left thigh and recite the tashahhud:
"At-Tahiyyaatu lillaahi, was-Salawaatu, wat-Tayyibaatu, as-Salaamu 'alayka 'ayyuhan-Nabiyyu, wa rahmatullaahi wa barakaatuh. As-Salaamu 'alaynaa wa 'alaa 'ibaad-illaah-es-Saaliheen. Ash-hadu anna laa ilaaha ill-Allaah, wa ashhadu anna Muhammadan 'abduhu wa rasooluh."

Meaning: All Words of Praise and glorification are for Allah alone, and all Prayers and acts of worship, and pure words and attributes. Peace be upon

you, O Prophet, and the mercy of Allah and His blessings. May Allah send peace and security upon us, and upon all of Allah's righteous slaves. I bear witness that none has the right to be worshipped except Allah, and I bear witness that Muhammad is His Slave and Messenger.

He should then send peace and blessings upon the Prophet Muhammad in the following manner:
"Allaahumma salli 'ala Muhammad wa 'ala aali Muhammad kama salayta 'ala Ibraaheem wa 'ala aali Ibraaheem, innaka hameedun majeed. Allaahumma baarik 'ala Muhammad wa 'ala aali Muhammad kama baarakta 'ala Ibraaheem wa 'ala aali Ibraaheem, innaka hameedun majeed"

Meaning: O Allah, exalt the mention of Muhammad and the family of Muhammad, as You have exalted the mention of Ibraaheem and the family of Ibraaheem; You are indeed Worthy of Praise, Full of Glory. O Allah, send blessings upon Muhammad and upon the family of Muhammad as You have sent blessings upon Ibraaheem and upon the family of Ibraaheem; You are indeed Worthy of Praise, Full of Glory."

He should then seek refuge from four things:
"Allaahumma innee a'oodhu bika min 'adhaabi jahannam, wa min 'adhaab-il-qabr, wa min fitnat il-mahyaa wal-mamaat, wa min fitnat il-maseeh id-Dajjaal."

Meaning: O Allah! I seek refuge with You from the punishment of Hellfire, from the Torment of the Grave, from the Trials of Living and Dying, and from the Trials of the Anti-Christ (Dajjaal).[5]

One should ask Allah whatever he wishes,[6] and desires from the good things of this life and next.

---

(5) The "Trials of Living…" are that which a person encounters in life with regard to being enticed by the worldly life and the desires to which it gives rise. The "Trials of dying…" are the trials of the grave, and the questioning by the two Angels. The "Trials of the Anti-Christ (Dajjaal)…" are the supernatural occurrences that will happen at his hands: things that will lead many people to go astray, to follow him and accept his claim to divinity.
(6) He may supplicate Allah in his own words, or native language.

12. Lastly, one should make the 'Tasleem' to the right, by turning his head to the right saying:

"As-Salaamu 'alaykum wa Rahmatullaah."

Meaning: May the Peace and Mercy of Allah be upon you.

Then he should make tasleem to his left, by turning his head to the left, saying "As-Salaamu 'alaykum wa Rahmatullaah."

13. If one is performing a three rak'ah Prayer, such as Maghrib, or a four rak'ah prayer, such as Dhuhr, 'Asr or 'Ishaa, after saying "Ash-hadu an laa ilaaha ill-Allah wa ash-hadu anna Muhammadan 'Abduhu wa Rasooluhu," in the Tashahhud mentioned previously, he should stand up and pray the third rak'ah for a three rak'aat Prayer, or the third and fourth rak'ahs for a four rak'aat Prayer. He should stand, while supporting himself with his knees if he is able, and raise his hands to the level of his shoulders [or earlobes] saying, "Allahu Akbar." He should recite Surah al-Faatihah. He should do the same as he did in the previous rak'aat. He should then sit for the last Tashahhud, completing it fully by sending peace and blessings upon the Prophet, and after its recitation, he should conclude his prayer by making the Tasleem.

VOLUNTARY PRAYERS

There are certain prayers known as as-Sunan-ur-Rawaatib[7], by which one would get extra reward and raise his level in Jannah. Through them, one makes up for any of his faults in the obligatory prayers, which have been mentioned in the table. The Witr prayer is also a sunnah prayer, and it consists of at least one rak'ah. It should be the last prayer one performs at night.

Forbidden Times of Prayer

Voluntary prayers, other than those mentioned, may be performed at any time other than those specifically forbidden by Allah and His Messenger ﷺ. These forbidden times are as follows:

1. After the Fajr Prayer until the sun rises a spear's length.[8]

2. The time just before and after the sun reaches its zenith until it descends a few degrees.

3. After the 'Asr prayer until the sun sets.

---

(7) See chart on p.42.

(8) About 15-20 minutes after the sun has risen.

08. ZAKAH

Upon becoming Muslim, one must pay Zakah to those who deserve it.

Zakah is a right from the rights of Allah which a Muslim must pay to his brothers from the poor and those in need to cover their requirements and save them from the humility of asking others. Allah says:

"And they were not commanded except to worship Allah, [being] sincere to Him in religion, inclining to truth, and to establish prayer and to give zakah. And that is the correct religion." [98:5]

There is a great wisdom and many reasons why Zakah has been prescribed. From them, may be the following:

The Conditions of Zakah: The elapse of one year. If one possesses the nisaab for a period of a complete year, Zakah becomes due upon him.

1. It purifies the souls of rich Muslims and cleanses them from greed, selfishness, base covetousness, and the love of this interim world and drowning in its desires.

2. It purifies the soul of the poor from hate and jealousy which they might feel for the rich. They see them giving from their wealth, and continuously caring for them, by giving them money and treating them well.

3. It causes a Muslim to grow fond of good manners, such as giving charity, and preferring others over himself.

4. It uproots poverty in the Muslim society and alleviates the dangers which result from it, such as theft, murder, and transgression against people's honor.

5. It brings the spirit of mutual dependence and Islamic brotherhood to life, by fulfilling the needs of Islam and the Muslims.

6. It plays a role in spreading Islam throughout the world. Through it, non-Muslims are shown the religion of Islam and its beauty, and it is hoped that they would accept it.

THE CONDITIONS OF ZAKAH

1. Possession of the nisaab, which is the amount of wealth upon which Islam has legislated Zakah. This amount is equal to 85 grams of gold.

2. The elapse of one year. If one possesses the nisaab for a period of a complete year, Zakah becomes due upon him.

THOSE ELIGIBLE FOR ZAKAH

Allah has specified those who are eligible to receive Zakah. Allah says:
"Zakah expenditures are only for the poor and for the needy and for those employed to collect [zakah] and for bringing hearts together [for Islam] and for freeing captives [or slaves] and for those in debt and for the cause of Allah and for the [stranded] traveler - an obligation [imposed] by Allah. And Allah is Knowing and Wise." [9:60]

IMPORTANT NOTES

1. There is no Zakah due on those items which one possesses for personal use, such as houses, furniture, cars, and beasts of burden (horses, donkeys, etc.).
2. There is no Zakah due on those assets one holds for rental purposes, like cars, shops, houses. Zakah must be paid on the rental payment if it is combined with his other wealth, reaches the nisaab and remains in his possession for a period of one year.

Zakah expenditures are only for the poor and for the needy [9:60]

THE FAST (SIYAAM) OF RAMADAN

Upon becoming Muslim, one must fast the month of Ramadan, every year. One must abstain from anything that breaks the fast; most specifically: food, drink, and sexual intercourse, from dawn until dusk as an act of obedience to Allah. Allah says:
"O you who believe! Fasting has been prescribed for you as it was prescribed for those before you, that you may become from the pious." [2:183]

The objective of fasting is not that one merely abstains from the material and physical things which break one's fast, but rather, one must also refrain from those intangible things which diminish [the reward] of one's fast; such as lying, backbiting, tale-bearing, cheating, deception, false talk, and other offensive behavior. He should keep in mind that it is obligatory upon him to abstain from these offensive things outside of Ramadan, but more so in this month, due to the saying of the Prophet ﷺ:
"Whoever does not refrain from false speech and deeds, Allah has no need for him to leave his food and drink." (Bukhari #1804)

There are many reasons and great wisdoms why Siyaam has been prescribed. From them are the following:

1. It is spiritual exercise for the believer, for his soul is making Jihad[(1)] against his wants and desires.

2. Keeping the Muslim's soul above all offensive speech and deeds. The Prophet ﷺ said:

The objective of fasting is not that one merely abstains from the material and physical things which break one's fast, but rather, one must also refrain from those intangible things which diminish [the reward] of one's fast; such as lying, backbiting, tale-bearing, cheating, deception, false talk, and other offensive behavior.

---
(1) Jihad: Here the word is used in its literal sense, which means "to strive against".

"When one of you is fasting, he should not speak evil, nor should he yell or shout, and if someone were to curse or fight him, let him say, 'I am a fasting person.'" (Bukhari #1805 & Muslim #1151)

3. Through fasting, one realizes how his needy brothers feel, and this encourages him to fulfill their rights, ask about their welfare, and look into their needs.

Ramadan Kareem

NOTE:
It is not allowed for a woman in her menstrual period or postpartum bleeding to fast until her bleeding stops. Once it does stop, she must have a complete bath (ghusl) and make up the fasts she missed. If one is ill or traveling, it is permissible for him not to fast, but he must make up those days at a later time.[1]

---

(1) One must make up the fasts before the arrival of the following Ramadan.

10. HAJJ

Upon becoming Muslim, one must perform Hajj once in his lifetime. Hajj is the pilgrimage one makes to the Sacred House of Allah (the Ka'bah) in order to perform certain rites at specific places at specific times. This pillar of Islam is obligatory upon every Muslim, male or female, who is sane and has reached the age of puberty, once in a lifetime if they have the physical and financial ability. If a person has an incurable disease which prevents him from performing Hajj, but has enough money, he must assign someone to perform Hajj for him. But if a person does not have enough money to fulfill his daily requirements or to support those whom he is required to support, Hajj is not an obligation upon him. Allah says:

"And [due] to Allah from the people is a pilgrimage to the House - for whoever is able to find thereto a way. But whoever disbelieves - then indeed, Allah is free from need of the worlds." [3:97]

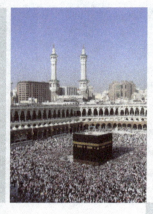

Upon becoming Muslim, one must perform Hajj once in his lifetime. Hajj is the pilgrimage one makes to the Sacred House of Allah (the Ka'bah) in order to perform certain rites at specific places at specific times.

There are many reasons and great wisdoms why Hajj has been prescribed. From them are the following:

1. To increase one's good deeds due to his act of obedience, for the reward of Hajj which has been accepted by Allah is nothing less than Jannah. The Messenger of Allah ﷺ said: "The 'Umrah[1] followed by another is an expiation for the lesser sins one performed between them, and there is no reward for a Hajj which has been accepted by Allah except Jannah." (Bukhari #1683 and Muslim #1349)

2. To realize the unity of the Muslims, for Hajj is the largest Islamic gathering. Muslims from all over come together at one place,

---
(1) 'Umrah: Lesser pilgrimage. It consists of Tawaaf and Sa'i whilst in the state of Ihraam. These terms will be explained later.

at one time, calling out to the same Lord, wearing the same clothes, performing the same rituals. There is no difference between the rich and poor, the noble and ignoble, the white and black, an Arab and non-Arab. They are all equal, except in piety (taqwaa). This is nothing but an emphasis of the brotherhood of all Muslims and the unity of their hopes and feelings.

3. It is a spiritual exercise which trains one to exert his efforts, physically and financially, in the way of Allah and seeking His Pleasure.

4. It is a purification of one's sins and wrongdoings. The Prophet ﷺ said: "Whoever performs Hajj (pilgrimage) and does not have sexual relations, nor commits sin, nor disputes unjustly, then he returns from Hajj as pure and free from sins as on the day on which his mother gave birth to him." (Bukhari #1274)

HOW TO PERFORM HAJJ

There are three types of Hajj; each one has its specific rites. The best type is Tamattu', wherein one performs Hajj and 'Umrah separately, in the Sacred Months of Hajj. It is done as follows:

1. One should enter the state of Ihraam[2] from the Miqat[3] before the 8th of Dhu'l-Hijjah. He should enter the state of Ihram, saying:
"Labbayk-Allahumma 'Umratan mutamitti'an bihaa ilal-Hajj."

Meaning: Here I am at your service, O Allah, performing 'Umrah and then a Hajj [separately].

2. After entering Makkah, he should perform Tawaaf[4] around the Ka'bah[5] and perform the Sa'i for 'Umrah[6], and then shave or shorten the hair. Women should clip her hair equal to a third of a finger's length.

---

(2) Ihraam: A state in which certain things become forbidden for a pilgrim.

(3) Meeqaat: Particular places which one cannot cross without entering a state of Ihraam if he wishes to perform 'Umrah or Hajj.

(4) Tawaaf: Circumambulating the Ka'bah counter clockwise.

(5) The Ka'bah is the first place which was made for the worship of Allah on the face of the earth. It was built by Ibraheem and Ismaa'eel, may the Safety and Mercy of Allah be upon them both, upon the command of Allah. Allah said:
"And Hajj to the House is a duty that mankind owes to Allah, those who can afford the expenses; and whoever disbelieves, then Allah stands not in need of any of the worlds." [3:97]

(6) Sa'i: The walking between the two hills of Safa and Marwa in remembrance of the struggle of Hajar, the wife of Ibraheem.

3. On the eighth day of Dhul-Hijjah, which is called the day of Tarwiyah, one should enter the state of Ihraam at the time of Duhaa'[7], from the place he is in. He should then go to Minaa', and there he should perform Dhuhr, 'Asr, Maghrib, and 'Ishaa' prayers. He should shorten Dhuhr, 'Asr and 'Ishaa' prayers [as a traveler does] but he should not combine them.[8]

4. After the sun has risen on the ninth day of Dhul-Hijjah, which is the Day of 'Arafah, one should leave Minaa' and head towards 'Arafah. He should pray Dhuhr and 'Asr at the time of Dhuhr, both two rak'ahs. After completing them, he should spend his time remembering Allah and supplicating him with sincere humility. One should ask Allah whatever he wishes raising his hands while facing the Qiblah.

5. When the sun sets on the Day of 'Arafah, one should set out for Muzdalifah. Once he has reached, he should pray the Maghrib and 'Ishaa' prayers, combining both prayers together, making the 'Ishaa' prayer two rak'aat only. He should spend the night in Muzdalifah. He should pray Fajr prayer in its earliest acceptable time, and then he should spend his time supplicating until the sky appears bright.

6. But before the sun has risen, he should leave for Minaa'. Once he arrives, he should throw seven pebbles at Jamrat-ul-'Aqabah[9], saying "Allahu Akbar" with each throw. The pebbles should be the size of a bean, or close to it.

7. After this, he should slaughter his sacrificial animal, and then shave or shorten the hair. Shaving is better for men, but as for women, she should clip her hair about a third of a finger's length. (She should never shave her head).

This pillar of Islam is obligatory upon every Muslim, male or female, who is sane and has reached the age of puberty, once in a lifetime if they have the physical and financial ability.

---

(7) Duhaa: Forenoon. The time after the sun has risen a spear's length until before it reaches its zenith.
(8) Allah has legislated that the traveler shortens the Dhuhr, 'Asr and 'Ishaa' prayers from four rak'ahs to two rak'ahs. A traveler may also combine the Dhuhr with the 'Asr prayer, by praying them together, one after the other, and the Maghrib with the 'Ishaa' prayer.
(9) These are three pillars in Minaa; the small, middle and large. The largest is the Jamrat-ul-'Aqabah.

8. With this one would partially terminate the Ihraam, and remain in a state of lesser Ihraam. He may wear normal clothes and do everything which is allowed for a normal person except for having marital relations with his wife.

9. One should then proceed to Makkah and perform the Tawaaf and Sa'i, both for Hajj. Upon completion, he should return to Minaa´ and spend the nights of the eleventh and twelfth of Dhul-Hijjah there. During the days, he should throw seven pebbles at all three Jamaraat, saying "Allahu Akbar" with each pebble. He should do so after the sun starts to decline from its zenith. He should begin with the smallest Jamrah, and then proceed to the middle and then the largest.

10. Once a person has thrown pebbles at the Jamaraat on the twelfth day, he may leave Minaa´ or he may spend another night in Minaa´, throwing pebbles at the three Jamaraat on the thirteenth day after the sun starts to decline from its zenith as explained earlier, this is more praiseworthy.

11. Once one intends to return home, he should proceed to Makkah and perform Tawaaf al-Wadaa' (Farewell Tawaf). This Tawaaf is not an obligation for a woman experiencing menses or postpartum bleeding. Once a person has done this, his Hajj is complete.

"And [due] to Allah from the people is a pilgrimage to the House - for whoever is able to find thereto a way." [3:97]

MY FIRST STEPS IN ISLAM

11. THE WORSHIP OF ALLAH

Know my brother that worship is obligatory upon every Muslim who is mentally sane and has reached the age of puberty. Performing these pillars of Islam is a means to enter Jannah, after the Mercy of Allah. The Prophet ﷺ once said to a Bedouin who came and asked:

"O Messenger of Allah, tell me what Allah has obligated upon me in terms of the prayer.' He replied, 'The five [daily] prayers, except if you wish to perform some voluntary ones.' He asked, 'Tell me what Allah has obligated upon me in terms of the fasting.' He replied, 'The month of Ramadan, except if you wish to perform some voluntary ones.' He said, 'Tell me what Allah has obligated upon me in terms of Zakah.' [The narrator] said 'So the Messenger of Allah ﷺ informed him of the legislations of Islam.' The Bedouin said, 'By Him Who has honored you, I will not do any voluntary acts, and I will not leave anything of what Allah has ordered me.' The Messenger of Allah ﷺ, said: 'He has succeeded (or, 'He will enter Jannah') if he is saying the truth.'" (Bukhari #46 & Muslim #11)

Know my brother that worship is obligatory upon every Muslim who is mentally sane and has reached the age of puberty. Performing these pillars of Islam is a means to enter Jannah

THE INDIVIDUAL AND SOCIAL EFFECTS OF THE WORSHIP OF ALLAH

1. The believers will achieve happiness and success in the life of this world as well as the Hereafter. Allah says:

"Indeed whosoever purifies himself shall achieve success, [as well as he who] remembers (glorifies) the Name of his Lord, and prays." [87:14-15]

2. Physical and spiritual strength which results from one's private conversation with Allah. Allah says:

"Truly, Allah is with those who fear Him and those who are doers of good." [16:128]

3. The Help of Allah and establishing His believing slaves' authority on the earth. Allah says:

"Verily, And Allah will surely support those who support Him. Indeed, Allah is Powerful and Exalted in Might. [And they are] those who, if We give them authority in the land, establish prayer and give zakah and enjoin what is right and forbid what is wrong. And to Allah belongs the outcome of [all] matters." [22:40-41]

4. Building ties of brotherhood, cooperation, bonding, and security between the individuals in an Islamic society. Allah says:

"The believing men and believing women are allies of one another. They enjoin what is right and forbid what is wrong and establish prayer and give zakah and obey Allah and His Messenger. Those - Allah will have mercy upon them. Indeed, Allah is Exalted in Might and Wise." [9:71]

5. The guidance of Allah and the success which is only granted by Him. Allah says:

"O you who believe! If you obey and fear Allah, He will grant you a criterion to judge between right and wrong, and will expiate for you your sins, and forgive you." [8:29]

6. An abundance of provision from Allah and ease in times of hardships. Allah

"And whosoever fears Allah and keeps his duty to Him, He will make a way for him a way out and He will provide for him from where he does not expect. And whoever relies upon Allah - then He is sufficient for him." [65:2-3]

7. A multiplication of reward and expiation of sins. Allah says:

"And whosoever believes in Allah and performs righteous good deeds, He will remit from him his sins, and will admit him to Gardens under which rivers flow to dwell therein forever, that will be the great success." [64:9]

MY FIRST STEPS IN ISLAM

12 THE COMMANDMENTS OF ISLAM

Dear brother or sister, seek a path in your relationship with society and others that is guided by the sayings of the Prophet ﷺ:
"Avoid the prohibited and you will be the best worshipper, be pleased with the sustenance Allah has provided for you and you will be the richest of people, be good to your neighbor and you will be a true believer, desire for others what you desire for yourself and you will be a true Muslim, and do not laugh much, for indeed laughing much causes the heart to die." (Tirmidhi #2305 & ibn Maajah #8081)

And he ﷺ said:
"A true Muslim is he from whom Muslims are safe from his tongue and his hand, and a true emigrant (muhaajir)[(1)] is one who abandons what Allah has forbidden." (Bukhari #10)

Islam aims to form a well-knit society, in which individuals show mutual mercy and love and exemplify the Sunnah of the Messenger of Allah by ordering them to do certain things and to abstain from other things.

Islam aims to form a well-knit society, in which individuals show mutual mercy and love and exemplify the Sunnah of the Messenger of Allah by ordering them to do certain things and to abstain from other things.

"The Believers in their love, mercy and feelings for each other are like one body: if one part feels pain, all the other parts feel pain by fever and sleeplessness." (Bukhari #5665 & Muslim #2586)

Islam has guided man to every good and warned them of every evil. Islam commands the following things:

1. It commands one to believe in the Tawheed (oneness of Allah) of Allah and forbids associating partners with Him (Shirk). Allah ﷻ says:

---
(1) The other type of hijra, or migration, is to migrate from the land of disbelief for the sake of Allah.

"Surely Allah does not forgive that anything should be associated with Him, and He forgives what is besides this to whom He pleases; and whoever associates anything with Allah, and he who associates others with Allah has certainly gone far astray." [4:116]

The Prophet ﷺ said:
"Avoid the seven destructive sins." They asked, "O Messenger of Allah, what are they?" He replied, "Associating partners (shirk) with Allah, sorcery, killing someone who Allah has forbidden without right, consuming usury, consuming the wealth of orphans, fleeing upon confronting the enemy in battle, and accusing chaste and innocent believing women (of committing immorality)." (Bukhari #2615 & Muslim #89)

2. It commands treating others well and forbids false consumption of wealth, such as interest, theft, deception, usurpation of property, and the like. Allah says:
"O you who have believed, do not consume one another's wealth unjustly but only [in lawful] business by mutual consent. And do not kill yourselves [or one another]. Indeed, Allah is to you ever Merciful." [4:29]

3. It commands justice and equity and forbids all types of oppression and transgression against others. Allah says:
"Verily, orders justice and good conduct and giving to relatives and forbids immorality and bad conduct and oppression. He admonishes you that perhaps you will be reminded." [16:90]

4. It commands that people cooperate in righteousness, and it forbids that they cooperate in evil. Allah says:
"Help you one another in righteousness and piety; and do not help one another in sin and transgression. And fear Allah. Verily, Allah is severe in punishment." [5:2]

5. It commands the preservation of life, and forbids killing and participating in it, except with due right. Allah says:
"Because of that, We decreed upon the Children of Israel that whoever kills a soul unless for a soul or for corruption [done] in the land - it is as if he had slain mankind entirely. And whoever saves one - it is as if he had saved mankind entirely. And our messengers had certainly come to them with clear proofs.

MY FIRST STEPS IN ISLAM

Then indeed many of them, [even] after that, throughout the land, were transgressors." [5:32]

Allah also says:
"And whoever kills a believer intentionally, his recompense is Hell to abide therein, and the Wrath and the Curse of Allah are upon him, and a great punishment is prepared for him." [4:93]

Islam commands well-treatment of one's parents and forbids disobedience toward them.

6. It commands well-treatment of one's parents and forbids disobedience toward them. Allah says:
"And your Lord has decreed that you worship none but Him. And that you be dutiful to your parents. If one of them or both of them attain old age in your life, say not to them the slightest word of disrespect, nor abuse them but address them in terms of honor. And lower unto them the wing of submission and humility through mercy, and say: 'My Lord! Bestow on them Your Mercy as they did bring me up when I was small.'" [17:23-24]

Islam orders the protection of the wealth of orphans and to treat them well, and it forbids consuming their wealth without right.

7. It commands joining the family ties and forbids severing them. Allah says:
"Would you then, if you were given the authority, do mischief in the land, and sever your ties of kinship? Such are they whom Allah has cursed, so that He has made them deaf and blinded their sight." [47:22-23]

The Prophet said:
"One who severs ties of kinship will not enter Jannah."
(Bukhari #5638 & Muslim #2556)

8. It commands and encourages marriage. The Prophet said:
"O young men!! Whoever of you is able to get married, let him do so, for it lowers one's gaze and keeps one chaste. Whoever is not able (to marry), then let him fast, for indeed it acts like a shield for him." (Bukhari #1806 & Muslim #1400)

It forbids fornication and homosexuality and all things which lead to it. Allah says:
"Say (O Muhammad): My Lord has only forbidden immoralities

THE COMMANDMENTS OF ISLAM

- what is apparent of them and what is concealed - and sin, and oppression without right, and that you associate with Allah that for which He has not sent down authority, and that you say about Allah that which you do not know." [7:33]

9. It orders the protection of the wealth of orphans and to treat them well, and it forbids consuming their wealth without right. Allah says:
"Verily, those who unjustly devour the property of orphans, they devour only a fire into their bellies, and they will be burnt in the blazing Fire." [4:10]

It forbids grieving and treating them badly. Allah says:
"So as for the orphan, do not oppress [him]." [93:9]

10. It orders that one be truthful in his testimony and forbids that one lie in them (*shahaadat-uz-zoor*). The Prophet said:
"Shall I not tell you the three greatest sins?" They said. "Indeed O Messenger of Allah." He said, "Associating partners with Allah (shirk) and mistreating your parents." He was leaning [when he mentioned that], and then he sat up straight (as if he was alarmed) and said, "And bearing false witness." [The narrator] said, "He continued to repeat this until we said (to ourselves), 'If only he would stop.'" (Bukhari #2511 & Muslim #87)

11. It commands that one fulfill his oaths and forbids that one lie about it, especially *al-yameen al ghamoos*, which means that one intentionally lies in his oath in order to deprive another of his right. Allah says:
"Verily, those who exchange the covenant of Allah and their [own] oaths for a small price will have no share in the Hereafter, and Allah will not speak to them or look at them on the Day of Resurrection, nor will He purify them; and they will have a painful punishment." [3:77]

12. It commands humans to take care of themselves and forbids suicide, whether directly or indirectly, such as dealing with intoxicants, cigarettes, and other things which modern medicine has proven to be causes of harmful diseases. Allah says:
"And do not kill yourselves [nor kill one another]. Surely, Allah is Most Merciful to you. And whoever commits that through aggression and injustice, We shall cast him into the Fire, and that is easy for Allah." [4:29-30]

13 It commands truthfulness, trustworthiness, and the fulfilling of oaths; and it forbids lying, deception and treachery. Allah says:

MY FIRST STEPS IN ISLAM

"O you who believe! Betray not Allah and His Messenger, nor betray your trusts while you know [the consequence]." [8:27]

14. It commands love and unity, and it forbids disassociation and all things which lead to hate and enmity, such as bearing grudges, hatred, and envy. The Prophet ﷺ said:
"Do not hate each other, do not envy each other, and do not turn your backs on each other (boycott), but instead be true slaves of Allah as brothers. It is impermissible for a Muslim to boycott his brother more than three days." (Bukhari #5718 & Muslim #2558)

Islam commands love and unity, and it forbids disassociation and all things which lead to hate and enmity, such as bearing grudges, hatred, and envy.

15. It commands generosity and forbids greed and miserliness. Allah says:
"And do not make your hand [as] chained to your neck or extend it completely and [thereby] become blamed and insolvent." [17:29]

16. It commands one to be frugal in all matters and forbids wastefulness and the squandering of money uselessly. Allah says:
"And give the relative his right, and [also] the poor and the traveler, and do not spend wastefully. Indeed, the wasteful are brothers of the devils, and ever has Satan been to his Lord ungrateful." [17:26-27]

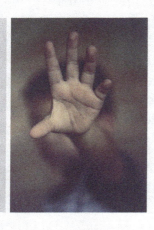

Islam commands people to console others and not feel happy about others' grief.

17. It commands moderateness and forbids fanaticism and extremism in religion. Allah says:
"Allah intends for you ease and He does not want to make things difficult for you..." [2:185]

The Prophet ﷺ said:
"Be aware and stay away from extremism in religion, for indeed the only thing which destroyed those before you was extremism in Religion." (Nasa'ie #3039 & ibn Maajah #3057)

18. It commands humility and forbids pride and arrogance. Allah says:
"And be moderate in your pace and lower your voice. Indeed, the most disagreeable of sounds is the braying of donkeys." [31:19]

THE COMMANDMENTS OF ISLAM

About arrogance, the Prophet ﷺ said:

"He who has even a mustard seed's worth of arrogance in his heart will not enter Jannah." A person asked, "O Messenger of Allah, a person likes to wear nice clothes and sandals. [Is this arrogance?]" He said, "Indeed Allah is Beautiful and He loves beauty. Arrogance is to reject the truth and to belittle others." (Muslim #91)

The Prophet ﷺ said about self-conceit:

"Whoever drags his clothes on the ground out of self-conceit, Allah will not look at him on the Day of Resurrection." (Bukhari #3465 & Muslim #2085)

19. It commands people to console others and not feel happy about others' grief. The Prophet ﷺ said:

"Do not feel happy about your brother's grief, it might be that Allah will show mercy to him and put you through a trial." (Tirmidhi #2508)

20. It forbids Muslims from interfering in affairs which do not concern them. The Prophet ﷺ said:

"Indeed from the good traits of a true Muslim is that he leaves that which does not concern him." (Tirmidhi #2317 & ibn Maajah #3976)

21. It commands respecting people and forbids debasing them and holding them in contempt. Allah says:

"O you who have believed, let not a people ridicule [another] people; perhaps they may be better than them; nor let women ridicule [other] women; perhaps they may be better than them. And do not insult one another and do not call each other by [offensive] nicknames. Wretched is the name of disobedience after [one's] faith. And whoever does not repent - then it is those who are the wrongdoers." [49:11]

22. It commands one to jealously protect and guard one's maharim[2], and it forbids that the person is not protective of his relatives and turns a blind eye to their promiscuity.

The Prophet ﷺ said:

"Three will not enter Jannah: one who maltreats his parents, a cuckold (Day'youth) and women who act like men." (Nasa'ie #2562)

---

(2) Maharim: Those relatives who are forbidden for a person to marry due to their closeness in blood relations, like mothers, sisters, aunts, daughters, etc.

MY FIRST STEPS IN ISLAM

23. It prohibits resembling members of the opposite sex. Ibn 'Abbaas said:
"The Messenger of Allah ﷺ cursed those men who imitate women and those women who imitate men." (Bukhari #5546)

24. It commands that people exert efforts in doing good to others, and it forbids that they remind them of their favors upon them. Allah says:
"O you who believe! Do not render in vain your charity by reminders of your generosity or by injury." [2:264]

Islam commands that people exert efforts in doing good to others, and it forbids that they remind them of their favors upon them.

25. It commands thinking good about others, and it forbids suspicion and backbiting. Allah says:
"O you who have believed, avoid much [negative] assumption. Indeed, some assumption is sin. And do not spy or backbite each other. Would one of you like to eat the flesh of his brother when dead? You would detest it. And fear Allah; indeed, Allah is Accepting of repentance and Merciful." [49:12]

Islam commands that one seek righteous companions and forbids that one seek evil companions.

26. It commands that one guards his tongue from all evil talk, and that he use it for good and beneficial things which would benefit himself and his society; such as remembering Allah, and reconciliation between people. Likewise, it forbids the individual to use it in evil. The Prophet ﷺ said:
"Are people thrown into the Hellfire on their faces or noses except for what their tongues have reaped?" (Tirmidhi #2616 & ibn Maajah #373)

27. It commands with well-treatment of the neighbor and forbids harming them. The Prophet ﷺ said:
"By Allah, he is not a true believer! By Allah, he is not a true believer! By Allah, he is not a true believer!" It was said, "Who is that, O Messenger of Allah?" He replied, "He whose neighbor is not safe from his evil." (Bukhari #5670)

28. It commands that one seek righteous companions and forbids that one seek evil companions. The Prophet ﷺ said:
"The example of a righteous and evil companion is like one who carries perfume and another who is a blacksmith. As

THE COMMANDMENTS OF ISLAM

for the one who carries perfume, he will either give you some perfume, you might buy some, or [at least] you will find a pleasing scent whilst with him. As for the blacksmith, either he will burn your clothes, or you will find a hideous odor from him." (Bukhari #1995 & Muslim #2628)

29. It orders people to settle their disputes and prohibits anything which leads to enmity and hatred. Allah says:
"No good is there in much of their private conversation, except for those who enjoin charity or that which is right or conciliation between people. And whoever does that seeking means to the approval of Allah - then We are going to give him a great reward." [4:114]

30. It orders that people be sincere to each other [by giving good advice] and forbids that advice be withheld when it is sought. The Prophet ﷺ said:
"The religion is sincerity and advice." We asked, "To whom?" He replied, "[Sincerity] to Allah, to His Book, to His Messenger, and [sincere advice] to the leaders of the Muslims and their general folk." (Muslim #55)

31. It orders people to help relieve the worries of others around them, to give them respite (in paying back debts) and to conceal their faults. The Prophet ﷺ said:
"Whoever relieves some worry of a believer, Allah will relieve a worry of his on the Day of Judgment. Whoever makes things easy for one in times of hardship [by giving respite to one who is not able to pay back a debt] Allah will make things easy upon him in this life and the next. And whoever conceals the faults of a Muslim, Allah will conceal his faults in this life and in the Hereafter. Allah helps his slave as long as he helps his brother." (Muslim #2699)

32. It orders that one have patience and fortitude in times of hardships, and forbids that one become worried and discontent. Allah says:
"And certainly, We will surely test you with something of fear and hunger and a loss of wealth and lives and fruits, but give good tidings to the patient. Who, when disaster strikes them, say, 'Indeed we belong to Allah, and indeed to Him we will return.' Those are the ones upon whom are blessings from their Lord and mercy. And it is those who are the [rightly] guided." [2:155-157]

33. It orders one to forgive, pardon, and turn away from one who does evil to him, and forbids that one seek revenge and retribution. Allah says:

MY FIRST STEPS IN ISLAM

"And hasten to forgiveness from your Lord and a garden as wide as the heavens and earth, prepared for the righteous. Who spend [in the cause of Allah] during ease and hardship and who restrain anger and who pardon the people - and Allah loves the doers of good." [3:133-134]

34. It commands mercy and it forbids cold-heartedness. The Prophet ﷺ said:
"Allah shows mercy to those who show mercy. Show mercy to those on earth, and Allah will be merciful to you." (Abu Dawood #4941 & Tirmidhi #1924)

Islam orders that people be sincere to each other [by giving good advice] and forbids that advice be withheld when it is sought.

35. It commands people to be kind and lenient to each other, and it forbids harshness. The Prophet ﷺ said:
"Nothing is done with kindness except that it is beautified, and nothing is devoid of kindness except that it is flawed." (Muslim #2594)

36. It commands that one return evil with good, and forbids that one reciprocate evil with evil. Allah says:
"Repel [evil] by that [deed] which is better; and thereupon the one whom between you and him is enmity [will become] as though he was a devoted friend." [41:34]

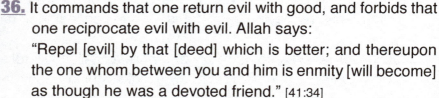

Islam commands people to be kind and lenient to each other, and it forbids harshness.

37. It commands the spreading of knowledge and forbids concealing it. The Prophet ﷺ said:
"Whoever was asked about knowledge but conceals it, he will be brought on the Day of Resurrection muzzled with the leashes of Hellfire." (Abu Dawood #3658 & Tirmidhi #2649)

38. It commands that Muslims enjoin virtue and righteousness and prevent evil and vice, each according to his ability. The Prophet ﷺ said:
"Whoever of you sees an evil act, let him change it with his hand, if he is not able, then with his tongue, and if he is not able, then with his heart, and that is the lowest degree of faith." (Muslim #49)

MY FIRST STEPS IN ISLAM

13. SOME PROHIBITIONS CONCERNING FOOD, DRINK AND CLOTHING

Islam prohibits alcoholic beverages and all drugs which lead to intoxication, whether ingested, inhaled or injected.

1. Alcoholic beverages and all drugs which lead to intoxication, whether ingested, inhaled or injected. Allah says:

"O you who have believed, indeed, intoxicants, gambling, [sacrificing on] stone alters [to other than Allah], and divining arrows are but defilement from the work of Satan, so avoid it that you may be successful. Satan only wants to cause between you animosity and hatred through intoxicants and gambling and to avert you from the remembrance of Allah and from prayer. So will you not desist?" [5:90-91]

2. Eating the meat of carrion, pigs, and all other things mentioned in Allah's words:

"Forbidden to you are carrion, blood, the flesh of swine, and that which has been dedicated to other than Allah, and [those animals] killed by strangling or by a violent blow or by a head-long fall or by the goring of horns, and those from which a wild animal has eaten, except what you [are able to] slaughter [before its death], and those which are sacrificed on stone altars, and [prohibited is] that you seek decision through divining arrows. That is grave disobedience..." [5:3]

3. Eating things over which the Name of Allah was not pronounced intentionally, or that over which other than the Name of Allah was pronounced upon slaughtering. Allah says:

SOME PROHIBITIONS

"And do not eat of that upon which the name of Allah has not been mentioned, for indeed, it is grave disobedience." [6:121]

4. Eating animals which have canine teeth, such as dogs, cats, lions, bears, wolves and the like, as well as birds which have talons; like eagles, falcons, hawks etc. Ibn 'Abbaas said:
"The Prophet ﷺ forbade us from [eating] any carnivorous animal which has canine teeth, and every bird which has talons [with which it catches its prey]." (Muslim #1934)

5. What was slaughtered by people other than Muslims, Jews or Christians. It is considered carrion and it is impermissible to eat.

6. Any food or drink which is apparently harmful to one's body, such as cigarettes and the like; they are impermissible. Allah says:
"And do not kill yourselves (nor kill one another). Surely, Allah is Most Merciful to you." [4:29]

7. Wearing silk, gold, and silver for men; they are permissible for women only. The Prophet ﷺ said: "The wearing of silk and gold has been permitted for the women of my nation, but not for its men." (Ahmad #19662)
It is allowed for men to wear silver rings, belts, and to use it for decoration on their possessions.

VARIOUS SUPPLICATIONS, WORDS OF REMEMBRANCE, AND ISLAMIC ETIQUETTES

14

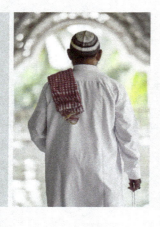

Greet both those you know and those you do not know by saying, As-Salaamu 'alaykum, for love and friendship would result from this.

1. Mention the name of Allah (by saying Bismillaah) before you start eating or drinking, and thank Allah (by saying Alhamdulillaah) upon finishing. You should eat from what is in front of you and you must eat with your right hand, for the left hand is mainly used to clean what is abhorred (like cleaning oneself after relieving himself).
'Umar bin Abi Salamah said: "When I was a young boy, I was in the care of the Messenger of Allah ﷺ and my hand was wandering all over the plate [while eating]. So the Messenger of Allah ﷺ said to me,
'Young boy, mention the name of Allah (before you start to eat), eat with your right hand, and eat from what is in front of you.'" (Bukhari #5061 & Muslim #2022)

2. Never be critical of food, no matter how it is. Abu Hurairah said:
"The Messenger of Allah ﷺ never criticized food at all. If he liked it, he ate it, and if he did not, he left it." (Bukhari #3370 & Muslim #2064)

3. Do not enter a house except after seeking permission (by knocking or the like). Allah says:
"O you who have believed, do not enter houses other than your own houses until you ascertain welcome and greet their inhabitants. That is best for you..." [24:27]

Do not persist in seeking permission more than thrice. The Prophet ﷺ said:

"One should seek permission thrice. If he grants you permission, then enter, and if not, go back." (Muslim #2153)

4. Greet both those you know, and those you do not know, by saying, As-Salaamu 'alaykum, for love and friendship would result from this. The Prophet ﷺ said: "You will never enter Jannah until you believe, and you will never believe fully until you love each other. Shall I not inform you of something that if you do it, you will love each other? Greet one another with 'Salaam.'" (Muslim #54)

5. If someone greets you with Salaam, return him the same greeting or one that is better.[1] Allah says:
"And when you are greeted with a greeting, greet [in return] with one better than it or [at least] return it [in a like manner]. Indeed, Allah is ever, over all things, an Accountant." [4:86]

6. When you feel like yawning, you should try to suppress yourself as much as possible. The Prophet ﷺ said:
"Yawning is from the Shaytaan. When one of you feels like yawning, let him suppress it as much as he can. And if one of you yawns, making the sound 'Aahh!', Shaytaan laughs." (Bukhari #3115)

If he is unable to suppress it, he should cover his mouth with his right palm. If he uses his left hand, he should either use its back, or make a fist and use the circle composed of his index finger and thumb.

7. When you sneeze, say, "Alhamdulillaah". If another Muslim sneezes and says, "Alhamdulillaah", you should reply by saying, "Yarhamuk-Allah (may Allah have mercy on you)". If someone replies to you by saying, "Yarhamuk-Allah", reply to him by saying, "Yahdeekumullaah wa yuslihu baalakum (may Allah guide you and better your affairs)". The Prophet ﷺ said:
"When one of you sneezes, let him say, 'Alhamdulillaah'. In turn, his brother or companion should say to him, 'Yarhamuk-Allahu'. And the one who sneezed should reply, 'Yahdeekumullaah wa yuslihu baalakum.'" (Bukhari #5870)

If a disbeliever says, "Alhamdulillah", you should reply saying, "Yahdeekumullaah (may Allah guide you)", only. (Abu Dawood #5038 & Tirmidhi #2739)

---

(1) If someone says, "As-Salaamu alaykum," respond with, "wa 'alaykum As-Salaam," at the very least. It is better to add, "wa Rahmatullaah," and even further, "wa Barakaatuhu."

MY FIRST STEPS IN ISLAM

Abu Hurairah related, that whenever the Messenger of Allah ﷺ sneezed, he would put his hand or his clothes in front of his mouth and lower his voice [in doing so]. (Abu Dawood #5870)

8. Do not burp in public. Ibn 'Umar said:
"A man burped while in the company of the Messenger of Allah ﷺ, and he said to him: 'Save us from your burping, for the most satiated in this life will be hungry for the longest time on the Day of Resurrection.'" (Tirmidhi #2478)

9. If you joke, do not say anything to harm or ill-treat others. The Prophet ﷺ said:
"Let not anyone take his brother's things (to anger him) seriously or jokingly." (Abu Dawood 5003 & Tirmidhi #2160)

Do not let your joking be untrue, leading you to lie to make others laugh. The Prophet ﷺ said:
"Woe to the one who lies in his speech to make people laugh, woe to him! Woe to him!" (Abu Dawood #4990 & Tirmidhi #2315)

10. When you wish to sleep, mention the name of Allah and lie down on your right side. Hudhayfah ibn al-Yamaan said:
"When the Prophet ﷺ would retreat to his bed, he would say:
'Bismika amootu wa ahyaa.'
Meaning: In your Name, I die and I live.
Upon awaking, he would say:
'Alhamdu-lillaah-illadhi ahyaanaa ba'da maa amaatanaa wa ilayh-in-nushoor.'" (Bukhari #5953)
Meaning: All praise is due to Allah, Who gives us live after He has caused us to die and to Him will be the resurrection.

11. When you go to your wives to have marital relations, say:
"Bismillaah. Allahumma jannibnash-Shaytaan, wa jannib-ish-Shaytaan maa razaqtanaa."
Meaning: "I begin with the Name of Allah. O Allah, keep the Shaytaan away from us, and keep the Shaytaan away from what you grant us [from offspring]."

When you go to your wives to have marital relations, say: "Bismillaah. Allahumma jannibnash-Shaytaan, wa jannib-ish-Shaytaan maa razaqtanaa."

Upon leaving your home, say the following supplication. The Prophet ﷺ said: "Whoever says upon leaving his home: 'Bismillaahi, tawakkaltu 'ala Allahi, laa hawla wa laa quwwata illaa billaah...'"

SUPPLICATIONS, REMEMBRANCE, ISLAMIC ETIQUETTES

The Prophet ﷺ said:

"If someone says when he approached his wife (before sexual intercourse), 'I begin with the Name of Allah. O Allah, keep the Shaytaan away from us, and keep the Shaytaan away from what you grant us [from offspring],' if Allah grants them a child, the Shaytaan would not harm him." (Bukhari #141 & Muslim #1434)

Also, keep whatever takes place between you and your partner private. The Prophet ﷺ said:

"Indeed from the worst of people on the Day of Resurrection is one who has marital relations with his wife and then spreads her private matters." (Muslim #1437)

12. Upon leaving your home, say the following supplication. The Prophet ﷺ said:
"Whoever says upon leaving his home:
'Bismillaahi, tawakkaltu 'ala Allahi, laa hawla wa laa quwwata illaa billaah.'
Meaning: I begin with the Name of Allah, I put my trust in Allah, there is no ability or might except with Allah.'
…it will be said to him, 'Your affair has been taken care of, you have been protected [from all evil], and the Shaytaan moves away from him.'" (Tirmidhi #3426 & Abu Dawood #5095)

13. When you visit the sick, invoke the supplication which has been narrated from the Prophet ﷺ. When he would visit the ill, he would sit close to their head, and say the following seven times:
"Asalullaah al-'Adheem, Rabb al-'Arsh il-'Adheem an yashfiyak."
Meaning: I beseech Allah, the Magnificent, the Lord of the Magnificent Throne, that He cures you.

He said:
"If Allah has written for him to live longer, he will be cured from this sickness." (Saheeh ibn Hibbaan #2975)

14. When you enter the toilet, enter with your left foot and say:
"Bismillah. Allahumma inni a'uthu bika min al-khubthi wal-khabaa´ith."

Meaning: I begin with the Name of Allah. O Allah, I seek refuge in you from the male and female Devils. (Bukhari #142 & Muslim #375)

When you leave the toilet, exit with your right foot and say:
"Ghufraanak."
Meaning: I seek your forgiveness. (Abu Dawood #30 & ibn Maajah #300)

MY FIRST STEPS IN ISLAM

15 BROTHERLY ADVICE

<u>**1.**</u> Know that upon entering the folds of Islam, Allah has effaced all your previous sins and evil deeds. The Prophet ﷺ said:
"Do you not know that Islam effaces all sin that is done before it?" (Muslim #121)

Rather, the evil deeds you committed before you entered Islam are changed into good deeds by the Bounty of Allah. Allah says:
"And those who do not invoke with Allah another deity or kill the soul which Allah has forbidden [to be killed], except by right, and do not commit unlawful sexual intercourse. And whoever should do that will meet a penalty. Multiplied for him is the punishment on the Day of Resurrection, and he will abide therein humiliated, except for those who repent, believe and do righteous work. For them Allah will replace their evil deeds with good. And ever is Allah Forgiving and Merciful." [25:68-70]

Those who embrace this religion from the People of the Book - from the Jews and Christians - will be given a double reward, due to their belief in their Messenger and their belief in Muhammad.

Listen to this good news from Allah. Those who embrace this religion from the People of the Book - from the Jews and Christians - will be given a double reward, due to their belief in their Messenger and their belief in Muhammad ﷺ. Allah says:
"Those to whom We gave the Scripture before it - they believe in [the Qur`an]. And when it is recited to them, they say: 'We believe in it. Verily, it is the truth from our Lord. Indeed we were, [even] before it, Muslims [submitting to Allah].' These will be given their reward twice over, because they are patient, and repel evil with good, and spend (in charity) out of what We have provided them." [28:52-54]

The Prophet ﷺ said:

"Whoever accepts Islam from the people of the two Books (the Jews and Christians) they will have a double reward. They will receive the rights we enjoy, and they must give the rights we give. And whoever accepts Islam from the pagans [other than them] will have their reward, and they will receive the rights we enjoy, and they must give the rights we give." (Ahmad #22288)

Your records are white and clean, so be careful not to taint it by doing any sins.

2. Now that you know the truth, set aside a part of your time to learn your religion. The Messenger of Allah ﷺ said:
"If Allah desires good for a person, He gives him understanding of the religion." (Bukhari #71 & Muslim #1037)

Seek the knowledge of 'Aqeedah (Creed) and then study everything else you need in your daily life about your religion, such as regards purity and prayer and all the rest. You should also study the rulings of trade and the rulings pertaining to your source of livelihood, so that you do not unintentionally fall into things which are impermissible. Also, try your best to memorize as much from the Book of Allah as you can.

You should understand your religion from its proper and trusted sources, the Book of Allah and the authentic Sunnah of His Messenger ﷺ.

Your example should be Muhammad ﷺ, and so you should strive to learn his biography so that you can emulate him. Try your best to be in the company of the scholars and students of knowledge who practice what they preach.

Be advised that not everyone who claims to be a Muslim is a true Muslim. Therefore, you should be careful from who you seek knowledge. Whatever you read or hear should be scrutinized in light of the Qur'an and Sunnah of the Prophet ﷺ And the Sunnah should be understood in light of the understanding of the early generations of Muslims. The Prophet ﷺ said:
"I advise you to guard yourself from the punishment of Allah [by obeying Him], hearing and obeying your leaders, even it be an Ethiopian slave[1].

---

(1) Slaves, regardless of their ethnicity, could never become leaders. Thus, this statement means that even if a slave became your leader by usurping the power, or taking it by force, you must nonetheless obey him to prevent chaos.

MY FIRST STEPS IN ISLAM

Calling to the religion of Allah (Da'wah) and his authentic Sunnah. You must be knowledgeable as regards what you call people to follow. In this manner, the doubts that the doubters of Islam bring about can be easily answered.

You must love and stand with the believers, and dissociate from the disbelievers and be cautious with them. But to do this does not mean that you have the right to oppress and transgress against them or usurp their rights.

For indeed whoever lives long amongst you will see many differences. So adhere to my Sunnah, and the Sunnah of the Rightly Guided Caliphs. Hold tight and cling on to it with your molar teeth. And beware of innovated matters [in religion], for indeed every innovated matter is an Bid'ah, and every Bid'ah is misguidance." (Abu Dawood #4607, Tirmidhi #2676 & ibn Majaah #42)

Whatever is in accordance with his Sunnah take it, and whatever opposes it, leave it.

3. Al-Wala and Al-Bara. You must love and stand with the believers, and dissociate from the disbelievers and be cautious with them. But to do this does not mean that you have the right to oppress and transgress against them or usurp their rights. You should not hate them, but rather your dislike should only be toward their disbelief and misguidance. This should encourage you to do your utmost to help save them from the Hellfire. Do not prefer disbelievers over Muslims, and do not help them against Muslims. Allah says:
"The believers, men and women, are allies of one another." [9:71]

4. Know that whoever accepts Islam would face opposition, disagreement and harm, especially from those closest to them. You should keep this in mind and know that if you are oppressed in any way, this would elevate your rank, purify your sins, and would serve as a test through which Allah is trying you to see the extent of your truthfulness and steadfastness on your religion. Allah says:
"Do the people think that they will be left to say, 'We believe', and they will not be tried? But We have certainly tried those before them, and Allah will surely make evident those who are truthful, and He will surely make evident the liars." [29:2-3]

Also, the Prophet ﷺ was asked:
"Which people are the most tested?" He replied, "The Prophets, then the righteous after them, and then those after

them. Every person is tried according to the strength of his religion, if his religion is strong, he is tested more, and if his religion is weak, his trial is lessened. A person continues to be tested and tried until he walks on the earth totally free of sin (for they would be effaced due to the trials)." (Tirmidhi #2398 & ibn Majaah #4023)

Know that they will try to raise doubts in your mind about Islam and constantly mention these doubts to you. Ask the People of Knowledge, so that you may find a proper reply to these doubts, from the Qur'an and the Sunnah.

5. Calling to the religion of Allah (Da'wah) and his authentic Sunnah. You must be knowledgeable as regards what you call people to follow. In this manner, the doubts that the doubters of Islam bring about can be easily answered. Give Da'wah as Allah says:
"Invite to the way of your Lord with wisdom and good instruction, and dialogue with them in a way that is best. Indeed, your Lord is most knowing of who has strayed from His way, and He is most knowing of who is [rightly] guided." [16:125]

Save others from the Hellfire, just as Allah saved you from it, and start with those closest to you. Be mindful of the words of the Prophet ﷺ:
"Allah did not send me to make things hard, rather as a teacher and to make things easy." (Muslim #1478)

Know that there is much good, and a great bounty from Allah in helping a person to become Muslim, The Messenger of Allah ﷺ said to 'Ali:
"If Allah guides a person through you, it is better for you than all that is on the earth." (Bukhari #2783 & Muslim #2406)

You will receive the same reward as all those who have been guided through you, without their reward being decreased in the least. The Prophet ﷺ said:
"Whoever calls to guidance, he will receive an additional reward equal to those who follow him, without their rewards being reduced in the least. Whoever calls to misguidance, he will receive the sin of those who follow him, without their punishment being reduced in the least." (Muslim #2674)

Know that conveying this religion to non-Muslims, and calling them to it, is a duty upon every Muslim, so do not fall short in doing this duty. The Messenger of Allah ﷺ said:
"Convey to others (the religion), even if it be one statement." (Tirmidhi #2669)

MY FIRST STEPS IN ISLAM

You should do your best to make people love the religion of Allah. The Prophet ﷺ said:

"Give glad tidings, and do not cause people to flee from the religion; make things easy for people and don't make things hard." (Bukhari #69 & Muslim#1732)

In calling others to Islam, you are not responsible for the results, for your calling is restricted to merely clarifying and showing people the way to the truth.

Know that in calling others to Islam, you are not responsible for the results, for your calling is restricted to merely clarifying and showing people the way to the truth. Allah says:

"And indeed, [O Muhammad ﷺ], you guide to a straight path. The path of Allah, to whom belongs whatever is in the heavens and whatever is on the earth. Unquestionably, to Allah do [all] matters evolve." [42:52-53]

As for the guidance by which one actually practices Islam, this is from Allah alone. Allah says:

"Verily! You [O Muhammad ﷺ] guide not whom you wish, but Allah guides whom He wills. And He knows best those who are the guided." [28:56]

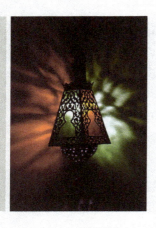

Try to choose righteous companions who encourage and help you to do good, as well as warn and prevent you from doing evil, and will be a support for you in your life.

6. Try to choose righteous companions who encourage and help you to do good, as well as warn and prevent you from doing evil, and will be a support for you in your life. The Prophet ﷺ said:

"The example of a righteous and evil companion is like one who carries perfume and another who is a blacksmith. As for the one who carries perfume, either he will give you some perfume, or you might buy it, or [at least] you will find a pleasing scent with him. As for the blacksmith, either he will burn your clothes, or you will find a hideous odor from him." (Bukhari #1995 & Muslim #2628)

7. Be careful not to go to extremes in the religion. There is neither monasticism nor fanaticism in the religion. Allah says:
"Allah intends for you ease and He does not want to make things difficult for you." [2:185]

Anas bin Maalik said:

Three people came to the houses of the wives of the Prophet ﷺ asking about the worship of the Prophet ﷺ. When they were informed, they thought it was too little and said, "Who are we in comparison to the Prophet ﷺ for indeed Allah has forgiven him his past and future sins." One of them said, "As for me, I will pray the whole night long." Another said, "I will fast every day without breaking it," and yet another said, "I will stay away from women and never marry." The Messenger of Allah ﷺ came and [when he heard of this] he said, "Are you the people who said such and such? As for me, by Allah, indeed I am the most god-fearing and most cautious amongst you, but I fast and I break my fast, I pray [part of the night] and I sleep, and I marry women. Whoever desires other than my practice (Sunnah), then he is not from me." (Bukhari #4776)

On the other hand, there should be no compromising or improper lenience in the religion of Allah. The Prophet ﷺ said:

"Indeed those before you were destroyed due to their [persistent] questioning, and opposing their Prophets. If I forbid you from something, abstain from it, and if I command you with something, do of it as much as possible." (Bukhari #6858 & Muslim#1337)

8. You will see many Muslims who do not fulfill their obligations and do not refrain from the prohibitions of the religion. People differ in this; such that some fulfill their obligations in a more complete way than others. In any case, the reason one does not fulfill these obligations is due to the fact that Satan is trying his utmost to misguide the Children of Adam. Allah, the Exalted, says:

"[So mention] when your Lord said to the angels, 'Indeed, I am going to create a human being from clay. So when I have proportioned him and breathed into him of My [created] soul, then fall down to him in prostration.' So the angels prostrated - all of them entirely. Except Iblees; he was arrogant and became among the disbelievers. [Allah] said, 'O Iblees, what prevented you from prostrating to that which I created with My hands? Were you arrogant [then], or were you [already] among the haughty?' He said, 'I am better than him. You created me from fire and created him from clay.' [Allah] said, 'Then get out of Paradise, for indeed, you are expelled. And indeed, upon you is My curse until the Day of Recompense.' He said, 'My Lord, then reprieve me until the Day they are resurrected.' [Allah] said, 'So indeed, you are of those reprieved. Until the Day of the time well-known.' [Iblees] said, 'By your might, I will surely mislead them all. Except, among them, Your chosen servants.' [Allah] said, 'The truth [is My oath], and the truth I say - [That] I will surely fill Hell with you and those of them that follow you all together.'" [38:71-85]

Do not be discouraged from fulfilling your duty in the field of invitation (Da'wah) to the religion of Allah. Let this be an incentive to yourself to strive in spreading the religion of Allah.

9. Practice Islamic conduct in your daily life; such as helping someone who is in need whether you know him or not, and smiling in the face of your brother. The Prophet ﷺ said: "Smiling in the face of your brother is a charity, enjoining good and prohibiting evil is a charity, showing someone the way when he is lost is a charity, helping the weak-sighted is a charity, removing a rock, a thorn, or bones from the path is a charity, and pouring water from your bucket into the bucket of your brother is a charity." (Tirmidhi #1956)

Your clothes and all your things should be clean. A Muslim must always be clean, for his religion is the religion of cleanliness. Allah says:
"O Children of Adam! Take your adornment at every masjid." [7:31]

You should try to do as many good deeds as possible, such as giving charity, performing voluntary (extra) prayers and other acts of worship.

When one performs these deeds [mentioned above] they are being an excellent role-model and example to the Muslims who are heedless of their religion. They will also serve as a shining ambassador to non-Muslims trying to

Practice Islamic conduct in your daily life, such as helping someone who is in need whether you know him or not, and smiling in the face of your brother.

You should try to do as many good deeds as possible, such as giving charity, performing voluntary (extra) prayers and other acts of worship.

understand the religion; since they would become curious and ask about Islam when they see its beautiful aspects before them.

Treat your relatives well, and do not sever your relationship with them even if they oppose your acceptance of Islam. You should have better relations with your relatives, in order to please Allah, and also as it may bring them closer to worshipping Him. They would also know that after you became a Muslim, your manners improved and you became a better person. Asmaa´ said: "My mother, who was a pagan during the life of the Messenger of Allah ﷺ, came to visit me, so I asked the Messenger of Allah ﷺ: 'My mother has come to visit me. Should I keep ties with my mother?' He ﷺ said: 'Yes, keep your ties of relation with your mother.'" (Bukhari #2477 & Muslim #1003)

10. Know that the struggle between good and evil will last till the Last Day. The weakness of the Muslims and the strength of the disbelievers, the minority of Muslims and the majority of the disbelievers, the backwardness of the Muslims and the advancement of the disbelievers, the humility of the Muslims and the might of the disbelievers are not evidences indicating the falseness of Islam. These are factors that change depending upon the era. There is no doubt though that the present circumstances of the Muslims are the result of their distance from implementing the legislation of their Lord and their abandoning of righteous deeds and calling to the path of truth.

'Umar ibn al-Khattaab, the second Khaleefah (Caliph) said: "We are a people who Allah honored and gave might through Islam. If we seek honor in something else, Allah would humiliate us. The truth should be followed..."

11. Know my brother that we are in the last of times (the Last Day is near) and that each year that passes, we come closer to the end of the world and the establishing of the Final Hour. The Prophet ﷺ said: "The time of my advent and the Hour are like these two fingers", and he joined his index and middle fingers. (Bukhari #4652 & Muslim #867)

The Prophet ﷺ foretold the state of Islam [and Muslims] in this time. He ﷺ said: "Islam started as a strange thing, and it shall once again return to this state. So glad tidings to the strangers." (Muslim #145)

Having many followers is not a proof of the correctness of a methodology. The Prophet ﷺ said:

"Glad tidings to the strangers! Glad tidings to the strangers! Glad tidings to the strangers!" Someone asked, "Who are the strangers, O' Messenger of Allah?" He said, "Righteous people amongst many evil ones. Those who disobey them are more than those who obey them." (Ahmad #7072)

He also clarified the state in which the Muslim who holds on to his religion will be, and the various hardships he will face (in practicing his religion), whether physical or psychological. The Prophet ﷺ said:

"Enjoin the good and forbid the evil, but when you see that greed is obeyed, desires followed, the life of this world playing its affect on people, and that people are pleased with their own opinions, stick to yourselves and leave commanding the general public with good, for indeed there will be days after you in which having patience in them is like grasping a hot coal. One who does righteous deeds in them will receive the reward of fifty of [the Companions]." (Saheeh ibn Hibbaan)

Know that all affairs are judged by the way they end, so be keen to always ask Allah that He keeps you steadfast upon Islam, and that He causes you to die with a good end.

12. Know that all affairs are judged by the way they end, so be keen to always ask Allah that He keeps you steadfast upon Islam, and that He causes you to die with a good end. Make sure your speech and deeds are purely for Allah's sake, that they are done according to what He legislated, and that you spend your time in Allah's obedience. Take account of yourself, before you are taken to account, and let Allah see you doing what He commanded, not what He forbade.

May Allah keep us steadfast on His religion, and cause us to die as Muslims.

THE MESSENGER OF GOD MUHAMMAD

An account of the life of Prophet Muhammad (peace be upon him). The book introduces us to the Prophet's noble character, his humble life and his conduct with his family at home, his companions and all people in society. It tells us how he strove to fulfil the task God assigned to him and contemplates how he dealt with his enemies, the exceptional magnanimity he showed to all and his simple, but highly effective, method of advocating his message.

THE KEY TO UNDERSTANDING ISLAM

This book explains how Islam is a code of living that covers all aspects of life. It comprises a set of acts of worship which play important roles in placing morality on a solid foundation and strengthening good qualities in people so that they are keen to follow the right path. The book cites many examples and speaks about the importance Islam attaches to knowledge. It mentions a number of recent scientific discoveries that the Qur'an has referred to 14 centuries ago.

THE MESSAGE OF ISLAM

The Message of Islam begins by reminding the reader that Islam, its worship, the rules governing people's transactions and all its teachings have always remained the same as they were taught by Prophet Muhammad (peace be upon him). No change or alteration has been introduced into the religion, though some Muslims have changed. The book discusses and sheds light on a number of rights to which Islam attaches great importance.

ISLAM IS THE RELIGION OF PEACE

Islam is the Religion of Peace, shows with perfect clarity that Islam is the religion of peace and that the spread of Islam means the spread of peace throughout the world. Muslims must always be true to their promises and covenants and treat others with justice and compassion.

EASE AND TOLERANCE IN ISLAM

This book explains that Islam admits no rigidity and making things easy is a general feature of all aspects of the Islamic faith. It is a religion God revealed that can be implemented by people with different failings, feelings and abilities. Islamic law takes all this into account and addresses human nature and appeals to it. God says: "He has laid no hardship on you in anything that pertains to religion." (22: 78)

HUMAN RIGHTS IN ISLAM

Human rights in Islam are outlined in the Qur'an and the teachings of Prophet Muhammad (peace be upon him). They aim to make man lead a life of compassion and dignity, so that he acquires all good qualities and deals with others in the best manner. The book clarifies the misconceptions that are often expressed regarding the different aspects of freedom and responds to criticism in a calm and objective way.

BILAL THE ABYSSINIAN

This book tells the history of Bilal ibn Rabah, a former slave who became a companion of the Prophet. The book expounds Islam's attitude to racial discrimination, highlighting significant events that show the Prophet took care of many of those who were persecuted, protected them and gave them their rightful status in the Muslim community.

THE PATH TO HAPPINESS

The Path to Happiness explains that the way of life Islam provides for its followers is divine and intended to ensure that people enjoy real happiness in this present life and in the life to come. Islam establishes the concept of true and everlasting happiness, which makes Muslims aspire to the sublime through obedience of God and earning His pleasure.

WOMEN IN ISLAM

This book discusses the status of women prior to Islam and how women were ill-treated and humiliated in many cultures. It explains how Islam put an end to all this injustice, established women's rights and gave women their rightful status.

ROMANCE IN ISLAM

This book highlights the great importance Islam attaches to love. It shows that the love of God is the best and the most noble love. When it is rooted in a person's heart, it sets that person's behaviour on the right footing, elevates his emotions and feelings and removes selfishness. A person who truly loves God extends feelings of love and compassion to all creatures.

ISLAMIC PERSPECTIVE ON SEX

This book discusses the Islamic approach to sex and how to satisfy the sexual desire in the proper and beneficial way. The proper way to satisfy sexual desire is within marriage and according to Islam, marriage is a necessity for the individual to achieve personal fulfilment. For society, marriage is the way to progress, development and stability.

JESUS IN THE QURAN

After first discussing people's need to receive the divine message through prophets, this book relates the story of Jesus, son of Mary (peace be upon him). It starts well before his birth, then goes on to discuss his message and the opposition he had to endure. The book also discusses the Qur'anic account of Jesus, which makes clear that he enjoys a very high position with God Almighty.

GLAD TIDINGS

Glad Tidings explains the nature of Islam and clarifies the error of people who rely on information on suspect sources. The book highlights the main features of Islam and tells everyone who embraces Islam that God erases all their past sins and errors. As the Prophet makes clear: "Islam wipes away all past sins."

MY FIRST STEPS IN ISLAM

This book explains for non-Muslim readers how to embrace Islam and shows that this does not require much effort. To new Muslims, the book explains the essential elements of Islam and outlines the character of Prophet Muhammad, his qualities and the message he delivered to mankind. It goes on to discuss the various acts of worship Muslims are required to offer, as well as their purposes and significance.

THE PURITY

Under Islam, the concept of purification is not limited to personal and physical purity; it includes purifying oneself of sin and all disobedience of God. This book discusses the detailed rules of physical purification, including ablution, grand ablution, the removal of impurity, dry ablution, etc.

HISN Al-MU'MIN

Hisn Al-Mu'min speaks of the causes of reversals and misfortunes that people encounter. It highlights how one can ensure the protection and preservation of God's favours and blessings, as well as preventing harm and reducing the effects of personal tragedies and calamities. The book teaches the ways and means to fortify oneself against the effect of such tragedies, the most important being remembrance of God and glorifying Him at all times. This book explains the best forms of such remembrance and glorification.

THE BEGINNING AND THE END

Questions of the creation, existence and progress of the universe have been raised by communities throughout the ages. Yet from its earliest days, Islam addressed these questions in a most direct and clear way. This book explains that the ultimate objective of creation is for all creatures to submit themselves to God and worship Him alone. All aspects of life in the universe inevitably end in death then will be brought back to life on the Day of Resurrection when they receive due recompense for their actions.

EVERY RELIGIOUS INNOVATION

This book defines and explains the various types of deviation from the essence of Islam and its true teachings. It reveals the negative consequences of deviation on Muslims and their life and how deviation is bound to give non-Muslims a distorted view of Islam. Finally, the book describes the role of Muslims in discarding all deviation, according to their abilities.

OsoulCenter
www.osoulcenter.com

IslamHouse.com

eDialogue
Interested in ISLAM?
Join For a Free Private Live Chat

edialogue org

For more details visit
www.GuideToIslam.com

contact us : Books@guidetoislam.com

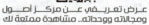
عرض تعريفي عن مركز أصول
ومجالاته ووحداته.. مشاهدة ممتعة لك

www.osoulcenter.com

To Download This Book, please Visit:

 OSOUL STORE